Managing the Historic Rural Landscape

The *Issues in Heritage Management* series is a joint venture between Routledge and English Heritage. It provides accessible, thought-provoking books on issues central to heritage management. Each book within the series is designed to provide a topical introduction to a key issue on heritage management for students in higher education and for heritage professionals.

Rapid changes are taking place in countryside management today, making their impact on the historic landscape. In an accessible format, this volume examines the questions and conflicts that arise in *Managing the Historic Rural Landscape*.

This volume:

- Confronts the major issues facing heritage managers today, such as evaluating what is significant in the landscape, the relationship of landscape management to the preservation of historic building, and issues arising when the landscape needs to be used for another purpose such as the contentious issue of the British Army's training centre located on Salisbury Plain.
- Presents these issues in a provocative case-study format – so that those actively working in the management of the historic rural landscape can provide context and explain the issues which are most important to their work.
- Provides case studies which are edited, introduced and commented upon to draw out most pressing and controversial issues for students.
- Brings together a broad range of perspectives from archaeology, ecology and government agencies to provide a comprehensive overview of policy and practice in the management of the rural landscape.

This volume is essential reading for students and professionals concerned with country-side management, in particular those involved with cultural landscapes, students of planning, agriculture, archaeology, ecology and heritage management.

Jane Grenville is a lecturer in archaeology at the University of York.

ISSUES IN HERITAGE MANAGEMENT
Published by Routledge in association with English Heritage

Series editor: Peter Stone, University of Newcastle

Managing the Historic Rural Landscape
Edited by Jane Grenville

Managing Historic Sites & Buildings
Edited by Gill Chitty and David Baker

Managing the Historic Rural Landscape

edited by
Jane Grenville

London and New York

First published 1999
by Routledge
11 New Fetter Lane, London EC4P 4EE

Simultaneously published in the USA
and Canada by Routledge
29 West 35th Street, New York,
NY 10001

Typeset in Bell Gothic and Perpetua by
The Florencetype Group, Stoodleigh, Devon

British Library Cataloguing in Publication Data

A catalogue record for this book is available from the
British Library

Library of Congress Cataloguing in Publication Data

Managing the historic rural landscape/edited by
Jane Grenville.
   p.   cm. – (Issues in heritage management)
   Based on papers presented at the seminar held
at the Society of Antiquaries, London in April 1997.
   Includes bibliographical references and index.
   1. Historic sites— Great Britain—Conservation
and restoration—Congresses.   2. Great Britain—
Antiquities— Collection and preservation—
Congresses.   3. Cultural property—Protection—
Great Britain— Congresses.   4. Historic
preservation—Great Britain—Congresses.
5. Landscape protection—Great Britain—
Congresses.   6. Great Britain—Rural conditions—
Congresses.   I. Grenville, Jane.   II. Series.
DA655.M24   1998
363.6'9—dc21   98–52377
                                                        CIP

ISBN 0-415-20790-8 (hbk)
ISBN 0-415-20791-6 (pbk)

Contents

CONTENTS

CONTRIBUTORS

Tim Allen The Countryside Commission
Ian Barnes Defence Estate Organisation (Lands) (South West)
Robert J. Cooke English Nature
Ian Dormor University of York
Graham Fairclough English Heritage
Jane Grenville University of York
Mike Griffiths Mike Griffiths and Associates
Peter McCrone Lancashire County Council
Helen Paterson Field Archaeology Division, Norfolk Museums Service
Clive Potter Wye College, University of London
Ken Smith Peak District National Park
David Thackray National Trust
Rachel C. Thomas English Heritage
Peter Wade-Martins Field Archaeology Division, Norfolk Museums Service
David Wells English Heritage
Tim Yarnell The Forestry Commission

LIST OF FIGURES

LIST OF TABLES

List of Tables

FOREWORD

This book is the first volume in the new series *Issues in Heritage Management*. The series, a joint initiative between the English Heritage Education Service (EHES) and Routledge, is based on discussions at seminars, organised and facilitated by the EHES, where those involved in particular aspects of the heritage were able to meet and exchange views, ideas and approaches. It is important to note that the seminars were conceived as educational, rather than policy-forming, events. They were intended to provide a 'snap-shot' of current policy and current practice and actively encouraged debate and positive criticism of the *issue* under discussion: they were not intended to put forward a particular English Heritage view or policy (although, as would be expected given the subject matter, English Heritage experts contributed to all of the seminars). As such we believe that the series will provide a useful and unique reference and introduction point for professionals, students and others interested in the heritage.

Most of the chapters in this volume are based on papers presented at the seminar *The Management of the Rural Landscape* although some additional contributions, identified at the seminar as being of major importance to the discussion, were especially commissioned. Inevitably, a single volume cannot hope to cover every aspect of the subject and some aspects of rural management are omitted from this volume, for reasons outlined below (see Grenville, this volume).

The seminar was held at the Society of Antiquaries, London in April 1997 and was organised by Jane Grenville and Ian Dormor. I should like to thank both Jane and Ian for all their hard work and diligence in planning and running the seminar. Without them it would not have taken place and you would not be holding this volume. I should also like to thank David Morgan Evans of the Society of Antiquaries, for hosting the seminar, Liz Hollinshead, the EHES Education Officer responsible for the series, for all her support, and Michelle Mulvihill, also of the EHES, who dealt with the administration of the seminar.

Peter G. Stone
Department of Archaeology, University of Newcastle, June 1998

LIST OF ABBREVIATIONS

ACRE	Action with Communities in Rural England
ADAS	Agricultural Development and Advisory Service
AHLV	Areas of Historic Landscape Value
AMAA	The Ancient Monuments and Archaeological Areas Act (1979)
AONBs	Area of Outstanding Natural Beauty
ASG	Archaeological Site Groups
BTCV	British Trust for Conservation Volunteers
CAP	Common Agricultural Policy
CAS	Wiltshire County Council's Archaeological Service
CBA	Council for British Archaeology
CCW	Countryside Council for Wales
CLA	Country Landowners' Association
CPRE	Council for the Protection of Rural England
cSAC	candidate Special Area of Conservation
CWS	County Wildlife Sites
DEO	Defence Estate Organisation
DoE	Department of the Environment
EC	European Community
EEC	European Economic Community
EH	English Heritage
ES	Environmental Statement
ESA	Environmentally Sensitive Area
ESG	Environmental Steering Group
EU	European Union
EWC	Environmental Working Committee
FA	Forestry Authority
FE	Forest Enterprise
FRCA	Farming and Rural Conservation Agency
FWAG	Farming and Wildlife Advisory Group
GATT	General Agreement on Tariffs and Trade
GIS	Geographical Information Systems

HBMCE	Historic Buildings and Monuments Commission for England
HMSO	Her Majesty's Stationery Office
ICCROM	International Centre for the Study of the Preservation and the Restoration of Cultural Property, Rome
ICOMOS	International Committee on Monuments and Sites
IEEP	Institute for European Environmental Policy
IFA	Institute of Field Archaeologists
IFS	Important and Fragile Sites
ILMP	Integrated Land Management Plan
LGMB	Local Government Management Board
LNR	Local Nature Reserves
LPA	Local Planning Authority
MAFF	Ministry of Agriculture, Fisheries and Food
MOD	Ministry of Defence
MPA	Mineral Planning Authority
MPG	Mineral Planning Guidance Notes
MPP	Monuments Protection Programme
NCC	Nature Conservancy Council
NFU	National Farmers Union
NMMP	Norfolk Monuments Management Project
NNR	National Nature Reserves
NPA	National Park Authority
NPPGs	National Planning Policy Guidelines
PPG	Planning Policy Guidance Notes
RCHME	Royal Commission on the Historic Monuments of England
RESCUE	the Trust for British Archaeology
RSPB	Royal Society for the Protection of Birds
RUPP	Roads Used as Public Paths
SAM	Scheduled Ancient Monuments
SMC	Scheduled Monument Consent
SMR	County Sites and Monuments Records
SNH	Scottish National Heritage
SPA	Special Protection Area
SPTA	Salisbury Plain Training Area
SSSI	Site of Special Scientific Interest
TAEM	Training Area Estates Management
UNESCO	United Nations Educational, Scientific and Cultural Organisation
WWF	World Wildlife Fund

INTRODUCTION

Jane Grenville

In the closing years of the twentieth century, we find ourselves at a critical moment in the development of agricultural and land management policies, nationally, on the European stage and globally. Since the Rio Environmental Summit of 1992, the buzzword has been 'agri-environmentalism', but the impact of changing emphases in policy-making reaches far beyond the agriculture and ecology implied in the new term, to embrace the cultural landscape. The aim of this book is first to outline the changes that have taken place and, second, to review responses to them in the form of innovatory land management systems. It is perhaps hardly surprising that in a fast-moving field where many interests are represented, there is not always agreement.

There have, of course, been earlier discussions of the relationship between archaeological and ecological conservation and agriculture. In 1977, the Council for British Archaeology collaborated with the Oxford Archaeological Unit to produce a statement of concern regarding the destructive nature of modern agricultural techniques (Lambrick 1977) and the concerns were raised by the Department of the Environment's Directorate of Ancient Monuments and Historic Buildings (the forerunner of English Heritage) a few years later (Hinchcliffe and Schadla-Hall 1980). By the late 1980s, the 'green debate' was in full swing. Archaeologists responded with a series of conferences to investigate the relationship between ecological and archaeological conservation. A very useful overview of the intellectual position at the beginning of the 1990s is provided by Macinnes and Wickham-Jones (1992) *All Natural Things – Archaeology and Green Debate* and amplified by *Rescuing the Historic Environment: Archaeology, the Green Movement and Conservation Strategies for the Historic Landscape* (Swain 1993). Management schemes that take account of both cultural and natural heritage were examined by Berry and Brown in their 1995 publication *Managing Ancient Monuments: An Integrated Approach.* Returning to the specific problems of agriculture and archaeology, a consideration of the impact on archaeology of environmental incentive schemes for farmers is offered by Dormor (1996).

To these twin intersections of archaeology with agriculture and nature conservation, we might now add the dimension of social perceptions of the countryside. This is an issue that is referred to either directly or obliquely by many of the contributors to this volume, and one which was brought home to us all in the UK by the Countryside March in London in early 1998: the analysis of conflicting images and political appropriations of the countryside is a plum ripe for post-modernist commentators to pick. A recent conference in York considered some of the implications of this diversity of view for the conservation and preservation of the cultural landscape (Dormor, Jacques and Mytum [forthcoming]). This book aims to update readers with current policy and practice in agriculture, environmental conservation and archaeological curation: the theme of dissonant social, political and professional perceptions runs as a thread through all these discussions.

How the book is organised

Clive Potter provides an essential introduction to changes in European policy that provide the framework for most of the work discussed in later chapters. European policy is beginning to move away from the provision of support for production, towards the provision of incentives that encourage the development of 'agri-environmental' policies: a theme taken up by several other contributors.

Management strategies are developing apace and in two major respects. First, statements of significance are increasingly being seen as fundamental to the effective management of historic places. These statements, interdisciplinary in nature, are integrated into management plans that take account of all available information and offer flexible and focused solutions to conservation problems. David Thackray of the National Trust describes these in more detail in Chapter 2. Second, there has been lively discussion over recent years regarding the efficacy of current management thinking, grounded in a system of designation in which archaeological sites, historic buildings, ecologically important sites, whole landscapes and so on, are legally defined and given protected status as Scheduled Ancient Monuments, Listed Buildings, Sites of Special Scientific Interest and National Parks. Graham Fairclough of English Heritage reviews the rationale behind this system of protection and considers some alternatives in Chapter 3. It is a theme that returns in later chapters: Robert Cooke addresses the issues as they apply to Sites of Special Scientific Interest, while Ian Dormor considers its implications for the archaeological resource. Helen Paterson and Peter Wade-Martins examine the usefulness of designation in a case study from Norfolk.

The second section of the book is concerned with the statutory situation. Ian Dormor has provided a comprehensive outline of the legislation and planning policy guidance as it affects the management of the countryside. The law is, of course, open to endless interpretation and the impact of legal provision is not always predictable, even in situations that one would have thought were clear cut. For instance, a recent debate in the pages of *Planning* magazine concerned the relative level of protection afforded to Areas of Outstanding Natural Beauty (AONBs) and National Parks. In response to an article about the recent failure of the South Downs to be awarded National Park status, a correspondent noted that the assumption that 'Areas of Outstanding Natural Beauty have the same status as national parks is quite incorrect' and goes on to detail the policy guidance offered by Planning and Policy Guidance Note 7 (PPG7) and statutory responsibilities of National Parks under Section 61 of the Environment Act. This is robustly countered by the author of the original article, quoting a press release from the Countryside Commission of 23 April 1998: 'Many of those people who thought that national park status was called for [in the South Downs] may be mistakenly believing that a national park offers extra protection. This is not the case: national policy gives the same protection to AONBs and to national parks' (*Planning* 1267, 12, 8 May 1998). The lesson for students of rural management is that both law and policy are open to interpretation and comment: one should attempt to keep abreast of developments and informed opinion. Law reports and planning appeal reports are particularly useful in this regard. Indeed, an article in the same issue of *Planning* (1267, 8, 8 May 1998) reports an early failure of the 1997 Hedgerows Regulations (see Dormor, this volume). Noting that the regulations protect hedges that are integral to field systems pre-dating early nineteenth century enclosure, the planning inspector at an appeal allowed the removal of a 220-year-old hedge, commenting that: 'Individual important hedgerows are not protected by this criterion unless they are necessary to the completeness of the whole field system. I must apply the regulations as I find them'.

Regulations and designations may, however, represent yesterday's solutions. The practicalities of the trend towards agri-environmental incentive schemes are considered by Peter McCrone, taking *Environmentally Sensitive Areas* as his case study. The original thinking behind this scheme came from the environmental lobby, and it is only latterly that explicit provision has been made within it for historic landscapes. McCrone's experience as the first archaeologist to be seconded to a predominantly ecologically driven scheme provides an interesting foray into the realms of integrated management, taken up again in the final section of the book.

In commissioning a set of case studies, it was decided not to revisit one area of study that has been given very extensive treatment recently, namely that of wetlands management (Cox, Straker and Taylor 1996), or to take case studies of individual sites or groups of sites (for which see Berry and Brown 1994 and 1995). Instead, specific users were identified: mineral operators, foresters and the Army. Also included here is a consideration of conservation practice in the National Parks. As Ken Smith describes, all the above-mentioned users are active in the Parks, but in addition he considers the tensions between conservation and exploitation created between the two primary users, the farming community and visitors in search of recreation. In each of these chapters, different stresses are highlighted. Mineral operators and the Army are necessarily and perhaps unavoidably destructive of archaeology in their activities, and yet as Mike Griffiths notes, quarrying provides prime research opportunities for archaeologists, whilst Rob Barnes makes the point that military use has preserved the archaeological landscape rather better than late twentieth century farming practices in the surrounding downland areas. In common with foresters, both users are able to predict with a high degree of accuracy their activities and, with the help of archaeologists and ecologists, assess their impact on the landscape. Control over visitor activities is a much less exact science, as Ken Smith notes. The latest fad, be it four-wheel driving along green lanes or scree running, may be enormously destructive, but control is difficult and these activities may cease as suddenly as they began: scree running at the Langdale Pike axe factory site seems to be yesterday's craze, as the runners have moved on to bigger and better slopes (Eleanor Kingston, pers. comm.). The unique Neolithic site may be saved from the most acute threat, but general visitor pressure and overgrazing by sheep continue, while the problem of major landscape damage caused by the scree runners is relocated rather than solved.

The final section looks to the future of integrated and community-based management schemes. Robert Cooke takes up Graham Fairclough's theme and looks beyond individual ecological site designations to consider the significance of the Character of England project initiated by English Nature and the Countryside Commission. The identification of a series of Natural Areas has major implications for total management whose significance could usefully be pondered by an archaeological community that is still, as Dormor points out, reluctant to grasp the nettle of whole landscape evaluation. This is all the more important given that there are vast lacunae in the coverage of PPG16, *Archaeology and Planning*, across the rural landscape, whilst Sites and Monuments Records by their very nature tend to be site specific, leaving the user to make the necessary connections between records. The introduction of urban databases constructed using Geographical Information Systems (GISs) in selected towns is an attempt to remedy this in the relatively confined space of the city, but what future is there for this kind of approach to the archaeology of the countryside? If the ecologists can do it, why not the archaeologists?

Within the well-defined boundaries of English Heritage's portfolio of Historic Properties, the integrated management of archaeology and ecology is well advanced as Rachel C. Thomas and David Wells demonstrate. It is interesting to compare the notion of 'Site Wildlife Statements', as discussed in Chapter 12, with Thackray's 'Statements of Cultural Significance' considered in Chapter 2. The intersecting interests of archaeological conservation, wildlife habitats and visitor satisfaction may present managers with problems of different type and degree. There are certain to be instances in which irreconcilable difficulties arise. Mount Grace Priory in North Yorkshire is one such case. This is a well-visited Historic Property, the remains of a Carthusian monastery which boasts, as an extra attraction, a reconstructed monk's cell, complete with replica furniture. Medieval monasteries were generally well served in terms of sanitation and water supply and Mount Grace is no exception. The good survival of the subterranean piping system encouraged two clans of stoats to colonise the site. The visiting public were oblivious of their existence until a television programme was made about them, whereupon they became celebrities in their own right, and visitor numbers at the site went up significantly. This may well have been to the delight of the property's administrators, but the pressure of stardom was too much for at least one family of stoats, which disappeared from the site as a result of the increased disturbance (James Lang, pers. comm.). Encouragement of visitors and good interpretation is part of good management, but at what price to the monument and its wildlife colonies is a moot point.

The potential for tension between archaeology and habitat maintenance is demonstrated by the badger problem at Thorton Abbey in Lincolnshire: here the animals were causing considerable damage to the archaeological deposits by building a sett within the earthworks. In the end, they were moved to a new home (James Lang, pers. comm.), although how to persuade badgers to agree to a relocation package remains something of a mystery to me – perhaps you have to make them think that it was their own idea. This tension between archaeology and nature conservation is most often raised in this volume in the debate over tree-planting. The disagreements over the wisdom of extensive replanting are argued vigorously from both corners. Cooke and Allen advocate increased tree cover with a tempered enthusiasm, but Fairclough and Smith, arguing from an archaeological viewpoint are more sceptical. Yarnell, an archaeologist working within a largely ecological context, provides a helpful commentary on the debate. Closer relations between the two professions, and the adoption of integrated conservation planning, should enable these disagreements to be addressed within a broadly agreed context, and problems to be solved on a site specific basis. It would be optimistic indeed to suggest that this process will ever be painless.

A striking aspect of the conference in London in April 1997 was that during the discussion periods many of the solutions to integrated management that were proposed seemed to be already in operation in Norfolk. The chapter from Helen Paterson and Peter Wade-Martins was one of those specially commissioned for this volume and describes various approaches to sustainable management of the archaeological resource. These range from designation, to outright ownership by the County Council, to detailed but voluntary management agreements with owners and tenants.

Finally, Tim Allen of the Countryside Commission returns the problem squarely back to its place of origin, the local community. The local significance of the landscape is often forgotten in the consideration of European, national and regional initiatives. Yet local perceptions of significance can never be ignored and the enthusiasm of local populations must be engaged if cherished landmarks and habitats are to be retained, for there are far too few professional conservationists to implement and oversee policy and projects. Perhaps more important, however, in this equation, is the centrality of the sense of ownership within local communities. It may seem trite, since the expression has been hijacked by political sloganeers, but unless there is a sense that the local population is a 'stakeholder' in the environment, then little can be achieved. Much of this sense of stakeholding is predicated by the 'idea' of the landscape. As hinted at above, this is an area that is of interest to sociologists, historians, geographers and political scientists, who have recently given much thought to the interface between landscape and identity (for example, Anderson 1991; Smith 1986 and 1991; Daniels 1993; Gruffudd 1995; Hobsbawm and Ranger 1983), all of whom seek to analyse the underlying issue of the meaning of national and regional identity. As Gruffudd (1995, 49) notes: 'at the core of this process of identification is the cultural and historical imagination – a profoundly fickle and fluid construct . . . It must be realised that . . . ethno-histories – encoded as 'traditions' – are frequently inventions or recycled myths.' The tensions between practical conservation, economics and ideology in the management of the countryside provide the subject matter of this volume.

A work such as this is inevitably a communal effort and acknowledgement of the major contributions of others must be made. Thanks must go particularly to my co-organisers. Ian Dormor was more or less single-handedly responsible for the arrangements for the conference and he handled them with his customary calm and efficiency. More importantly, his academic input in the planning stages was essential and it is to him that we owe the broad remit of this volume, which under my sole guidance would have been much the poorer for the lack of insights from those concerned with countryside management beyond archaeology. His help with the editing process has been invaluable. Peter Stone, the series editor, has been a voice of calm and sound advice throughout. Graham Fairclough co-chaired the conference on the day and has been a source of helpful comment since. My thanks go also to all the contributors, particularly those who sent their papers promptly, but also to the latecomers who submitted with good humour to telephonic and epistolary handbaggings (and, indeed, in one case to a personal confrontation when unable to avoid me in a lunch queue at a subsequent conference!). Vicky Peters at Routledge and the staff of English Heritage's Photo Library have provided helpful last minute support. Finally my special thanks to Barbara Wills for practical and moral support which may appear to be taken for granted, but isn't.

■ ■ ■

References

Anderson, B. (1991) *Imagined Communities: Reflections on the Origins and Spread of Nationalism*, London: Verso.

Berry, A. and Brown, I. (1994) *Erosion of Archaeological Earthworks: Its Prevention, Control and Repair*, Mold: Clwyd Archaeological Service in association with Association of County Archaeology Officers

—— (1995) *Managing Ancient Monuments: An Integrated Approach,* Mold: Clwyd Archaeological Service in association with Association of County Archaeology Officers.

Cox, M., Straker, V. and Taylor, D. (eds) (1996) *Wetlands Archaeology and Conservation,* London: HMSO.

Daniels, S. (1993) *Fields of Vision: Landscape Imagery and National Identity in England and the United States,* Cambridge: Polity Press.

Dormor, I. (1996) 'An Appraisal of the Archaeological Potential of Farming Incentive Schemes' in J. Grenville (ed.) *Archaeological Heritage Management and the English Agricultural Landscape,* York Archaeological Heritage Studies, Occasional Paper 1, York: Department of Archaeology, University of York.

Dormor, I., Jacques, D. and Mytum, H. (forthcoming) *Interpreting Historic Places: Myths, Images and Identity,* proceedings of a conference held in York, September 1997, Shaftesbury: Donhead.

Gruffudd, P. (1995) 'Heritage as National Identity' in David. T. Herbert (ed.) *Heritage, Tourism and Society,* London: Pinter.

Hinchcliffe, J. and Schadla-Hall, T. (1980) *The Past under the Plough,* Directorate of Ancient Monuments and Historic Buildings, Occasional Paper 3, London: Department of the Environment.

Hobsbawm, E. and Ranger, T. (1983) *The Invention of Tradition,* Cambridge: Cambridge University Press.

Lambrick, G. (1977) *Archaeology and Agriculture,* Oxford: Council for British Archaeology and the Oxford Archaeological Unit.

Macinnes, L. and Wickham-Jones, C.R. (1992) *All Natural Things – Archaeology and Green Debate,* Oxbow Monograph 21, Oxford: Oxbow.

Planning for the Natural and Built Environment, incorporating Planning Week, London: Planning Publishers Ltd.

Smith, A.D. (1986) *The Ethnic Origins of Nations,* Oxford: Basil Blackwell.

—— (1991) *National Identity,* Harmondsworth: Penguin Books.

Swain, H. (ed) (1993) *Rescuing the Historic Environment: Archaeology, the Green Movement and Conservation Strategies for the British Landscape,* Hereford: RESCUE.

PART ONE

Policy Background

Chapter 1

DEFINING THE RURAL POLICY CONTEXT

Clive Potter

Introduction

For most of the last 40 years, the policy framework for historic landscape conservation in Britain has been overwhelmingly an agricultural one. It is certainly true that agricultural support, first under domestic UK farming policies, and since 1973, under the European Union's Common Agricultural Policy (CAP), has absorbed the lion's share of government spending in the countryside. This has had a profound effect on the use and management of rural land, to the extent that contemplating a future without the CAP (as policy-makers are now beginning to do) requires rethinking the whole rural policy scene. This chapter describes the way the CAP has not only shaped the appearance of the post-war countryside but also limited attempts to conserve what is left. It goes on to explain how, from the mid 1980s, the invention of what has become known as 'agri-environmental policy' improved the incentives for landscape conservation in Britain and assesses what has been achieved as a result of this policy shift. The chapter concludes with a look forward to accelerating international agricultural policy reform, and the ushering in of a European rural policy; these may bring about a still more radical (and even more environmentally useful) rearrangement of the rural policy scene.

An engine of destruction?

Not all commentators agree that the CAP has been, to use William Waldegrave's phrase, an 'engine of destruction' in Britain's countryside since the war. Admittedly, the causes and processes of landscape change are complicated and there is something in the argument that, even without the inducement of unlimited price guarantees, technological changes in agriculture would still have required the transformation of the lowland enclosure landscape. As Cheshire (1985) points out, however, it cannot be immaterial that the invention of the CAP in the early 1960s created an economic environment offering price levels undreamt of by most European farmers. The most convincing explanations of recent landscape change remain those that are strongly policy driven. In effect, farmers responded to high prices and unlimited markets for their products, by intensifying production in order to maximise their policy receipts. From the mid 1960s, farmers throughout north-west Europe started to abandon the mixed farming systems that had produced the traditional bocage-type landscape of small enclosures. Indeed, the removal of hedgerows to facilitate large-scale and more specialised farming operations was arguably the first visible sign of gathering agri-environmental change, not just in the UK but in Denmark, Belgium and northern France (Potter 1998). In the UK, publication of the Countryside Commission's *New Agricultural Landscapes* study (Westmacott and Worthington 1974) brought home the extent to which agricultural intensification was sweeping away many of the features of traditional landscapes. Later, the Nature Conservancy Council made this bleak assessment of the prospects for wildlife in Britain's countryside under the CAP:

> While a few habitats that are rich in wildlife are increasing, most in the intensively farmed parts of Britain are declining in size, quality, or both. The decline is serious: it is occurring throughout the lowlands and more fertile uplands of England, Wales and Scotland . . . the rate and extent of change during the last thirty five years is greater than at any similar length of time in history.
>
> (Nature Conservancy Council 1977: 21)

In retrospect, this was a significant admission for one of the Government's statutory conservation advisers to make, for it signalled the failure of post-war conservation policy to defend agricultural landscapes as a conservation resource and was to have profound implications for the future evolution of policy. Until this point, nature conservation had chiefly been seen as an enterprise of selecting and designating National Nature Reserves (NNRs) and Sites of Special Scientific Interest (SSIs). As Felton (1993) observes, the luxury of being able to present nature conservation as a largely scientific and educational project, centred on the selection, management and protection of key sites, was only possible because a prescribed form of countryside management was not deemed to be required elsewhere. This of course had been the message of the famous Scott Committee on Land Utilisation in Rural Areas (Scott 1942), which had opined that 'even if there were no economic, social or strategic reason for the maintenance of agriculture, the cheapest, indeed the only way, of preserving the countryside in anything like its traditional aspect would still be to farm it'. The Scott philosophy became the touchstone of rural planning, justifying a dual approach to rural land-use management which combined strict development control under the town and country planning system to safeguard productive agricultural land, with an expansionist farm support policy bereft of any environmental safeguards. For the next 30 years, conservationists would devote much of their energy to creating a conservation estate made up of National Parks, NNRs and SSSIs; they would have little interest in influencing the course of change in the wider countryside, and few powers to do so.

Greening the CAP

By the time the Nature Conservancy Council came to publish the report quoted above, however, attitudes towards agriculture were hardening. With growing recognition of the destructive potential of modern agricultural practices and of the role of the CAP in accelerating landscape change, various proposals were made for 'greening the CAP'. It was widely agreed that the priority should be to improve the economic incentive for farmers to manage and conserve landscape features and habitats on their farms, and that the best way to do this would be to switch expenditure from production support into environmental schemes. The first sign that the Ministry of Agriculture was beginning to take seriously this simple but powerful idea came in the Norfolk Broads. Here an experimental scheme was set up in 1984 to pay farmers within the Halvergate Marshes, one of the last remaining stretches of traditionally managed grazing marshes in eastern England, to continue farming in an environmentally friendly way. Later, MAFF sought an amendment to an EC Regulation to enable agriculture departments to designate 'Environmentally Sensitive Areas' (ESAs), within which farmers would be offered what amounted to environmental land management contracts designed to protect habitat and maintain landscape (see McCrone, this volume). Since then ESAs have become an established part of the rural policy scene, covering over 1,000,000 hectares in England. Their significance is twofold. First, they have brought about a large extension in the conservation estate, bringing many more farmers into conservation than was possible before. Farmers have evidently found ESA agreements attractive propositions and, although ESA participation rates are variable (see Figure 1.1), the 400,000 hectares voluntarily enrolled to date is a good achievement. Second, ESAs are financed directly from the agriculture budget. This is an environmental scheme operated by agriculture departments, an institutional combination agri-environmental reformers have long been pushing for.

Assessing the environmental performance of ESAs has nevertheless not been easy and, more than a decade after the programme's introduction, is still an imperfect art. Countryside management to maintain and improve the ecological, aesthetic and historic landscape value of farmland is a complex, long-term undertaking which cannot easily be reduced to quantifiable outputs. MAFF's own assessments show that ESAs have been most successful in maintaining the environmental capital which

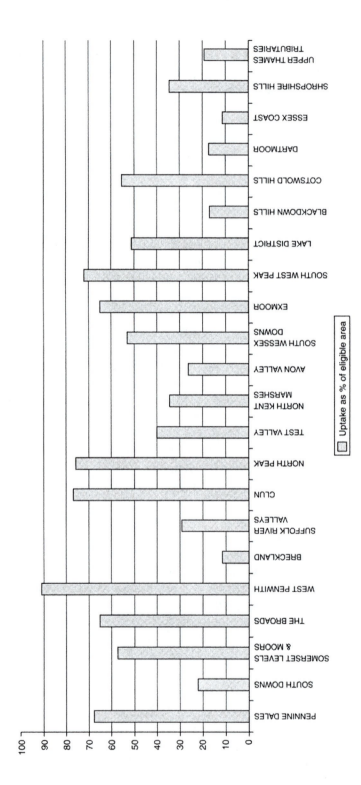

Figure 1.1 ESA uptake as a proportion of eligible area (management tiers combined)

Source: Compiled from unpublished MAFF uptake data

already exists on farms but have been much less effective in adding to or enhancing that capital. In the Pennine Dales, for instance, the ESA has been credited with cutting fertiliser use on upland farms but in the North Peak the impact on land use has been slight. In the Broads ESA, agreements have reversed the trend towards converting grassland to arable. In the South Downs, they have helped maintain upland chalk grassland and achieved some reconversion of arable back to grass (the recent case of a farmer deciding to plough up ESA grassland notwithstanding), but they have had a much more marginal impact on the conservation of habitat mosaics in the river valleys.

All that said, a decade after the first ESAs were designated, the attitudes of policy-makers and lobbyists are still remarkably upbeat. At the very least, the scheme seems to have drawn some of the sting of the Ministry's critics. MAFF has set up what is arguably one of the most comprehensive systems of conservation incentives of any EU Member State and is committed to making further improvements and refinements as time goes on. Nevertheless, the support of many conservationists for the ESA programme has always been provisional. It was assumed by groups like the Council for the Protection of Rural England (CPRE) and the Royal Society for the Protection of Birds (RSPB), for instance, that the ESA programme was an experiment, albeit a rather elaborate one, and that the ultimate desideratum is a system which would offer a conservation incentive to all farmers and land managers, whether they farm in an 'environmentally sensitive area' or not. It was against this background that the Countryside Stewardship Scheme was developed, being designed to complement ESAs by offering farmers in the wider countryside incentives for management and restoration. As the Countryside Commission, the originator of the scheme before its recent handover to MAFF, put it 'environmentally friendly farming needs special incentives in all parts of the country, not just in areas with nationally important landscape types' (Countryside Commission 1989: 3). Under the Countryside Stewardship Scheme in England, and its sister Tir Cymen scheme in Wales (Countryside Council for Wales 1992), farmers have been offered ten-year agreements for the purposes of landscape restoration and access improvement. Despite comparatively modest funding (total expenditure on Stewardship in 1996 was £17 million compared to £49 million on ESAs), high uptake rates have been reported in all the target landscapes, some 92,000 hectares having been enrolled by the spring of 1996 (see Figure 1.2). Meanwhile, other experimental 'agri-environmental' schemes have been set up under the agreement by European farm ministers in 1992 that all Member States should have an agri-environmental programme and that this should be eligible for EU support.

The question many conservationists are beginning to ask themselves is whether the resulting suite of agri-environmental schemes is doing enough to ensure the protection of the conservation resource. Even if regarded as pilots for some more ambitious arrangement which could one day replace the existing system of production subsidies, for the present they cut against the grain of a CAP still

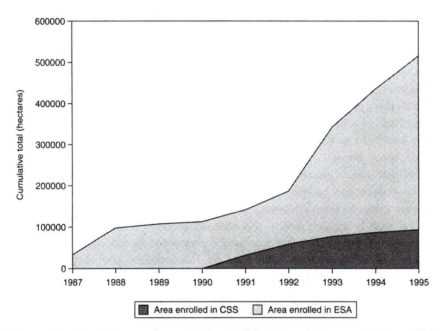

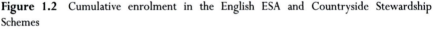

Figure 1.2 Cumulative enrolment in the English ESA and Countryside Stewardship Schemes

Source: Compiled from unpublished MAFF uptake data

overwhelmingly dedicated to encouraging increases in output or compensating farmers for the modest cuts in price support that have so far been achieved. Expenditure on price support still massively outweighs the small sums available for agri-environmental schemes (just three per cent of total agricultural spending at EU level in 1996). Total spending on the Countryside Stewardship Scheme was worth less than the subsidy on oilseed rape available to English farmers in that year. This imbalance not only makes it more difficult to attract enough farmers into voluntary schemes to make a difference: it also maintains the incentive for intensification on the land not enrolled in schemes. Evidence from the Countryside Survey 1990 suggests a continuing loss of biodiversity on arable land and an acceleration of hedgerow loss during the later 1980s. If anything, standards of countryside management outside ESAs have declined, with an increase in the length on 'non-stockproof' hedges and further deteriorations in woodland management (Barr *et al.* 1993).

The long game

Even so, it is now widely assumed that, as policy-makers finally set about reform of the CAP, the future will see the steady expansion of agri-environmental schemes at the expense of production support. Significantly, the pressures for this originate from international rather than domestic sources and are thus less likely to be 'finessed' in the way budgetary pressures have been in the past – or so the experts on the CAP would have us believe! Following the conclusion of the last round of negotiations of the General Agreement on Tariffs and Trade (GATT), policy-makers agreed that protectionist agricultural policies like the CAP had to be reformed in the interests of freer world trade. Signatories to the GATT Uruguay Round Agriculture Agreement (including EU representatives) agreed to the progressive decoupling of financial support from decisions about production. Where farmers continue to receive government support, this should be done in the least trade-distorting way possible. As one commentator puts it 'The Uruguay Round GATT Agreement arranged the straitjacket around the CAP. The next round (scheduled to commence in 1999) will tighten the cords and begin the painful process of dismantling CAP support' (Swinbank 1996).

If this is so, then European farmers may be about to undergo one of the most decisive reductions in agricultural support for four decades. The implications for rural land use and for the conservation of historic landscapes are profound. To begin with, a reduction in production subsidies should of itself bring about a relocation and extensification of production and, it is claimed, reduce pressure on the conservation resource. Economists predict that an immediate effect of a cut in price support should be to reduce incentives for farmers to use land-saving technologies and farming inputs. The theoretical argument is that a cut in price support will depress land values and rents, making it less necessary for farmers to economise in their use of the land input by applying more fertilisers and pesticides to every hectare of land in production. It is widely assumed that the resulting extensification of production will be good for the environment, reducing surface and groundwater pollution, eliminating overgrazing and easing pressure to reclaim land from semi-natural vegetation.

On the other hand, it is far from clear that historic landscapes and habitats requiring management would necessarily benefit from a withdrawal of support and a reduction in the profitability of farming, especially in more marginal areas. Two observations can be made here. First, there is likely to be a relationship between the pace of reform and the nature of any associated environmental impact. A rapid withdrawal of support (politically very unlikely) would give rise to the most dramatic changes in land use and countryside character, as falling land values and tighter margins drove some farmers out of business and brought about a restructuring of production. The phased reduction in price support over a number of years (now signalled by the European Commission's Agenda 2000 proposals) suggests a more complicated picture as farmers adjust to a new economic environment. If the general forecasts are right, a gradual liberalisation of the CAP will bring about a contraction in Europe's farm output as world production gravitates towards countries and regions with greater comparative advantage, particularly in the production of dairy products and cereals. For a Member State like the UK, the drawing back of arable production to the best land in East Anglia, the East Midlands and parts of the south would have many environmental consequences, chiefly connected with a shift out of tillage and into grass. Elsewhere there may be movements of land out of farming altogether and into forestry and industrial crops. Farm businesses already 'on the edge' economically would likely disappear before enterprise adjustments could be made and the land released bought up by neighbouring farmers, private forestry companies and, conceivably, conservation groups and trusts. Many commentators conclude from all this that the nature conservation effects of reducing price support do not all run in the same direction and that a redirection of support into expanded agri-environmental programmes is essential if farmers are to be provided with sufficient incentive to manage the countryside. The case for special assistance to keep high natural value farming systems in place would seem to be well made, for it could (and will) be argued that, without it, liberalisation will wipe out much of the human capital necessary for the effective management and conservation of the countryside. The main sources of uncertainty here are political. To what extent will taxpayers be prepared to pay for such an expansion in green programmes, especially when the benefits may be hard to quantify and slow to appear? The most likely evolution of EU policy will involve the attachment of progressively more restrictive environmental conditions to any income and compensation payments made during a long transition to a more liberal market regime. This could eventually give way to a permanent system of 'green box' entitlements (subsidies deemed to be non-trade distorting and thus allowable under GATT rules) that would be offered to farmers under some sort of European Rural Policy.

What is clear is that agri-environmental reform is far from complete and still has some way to run. Policy logic and World Trading Organisation rules, to say nothing of shifting public opinion, suggest that green payments will be one of the few politically sustainable ways to support agriculture in the years ahead and that agri-environmental policy looks set to become a key part of the rural policy scene. It defines the larger policy context in which the management and conservation of historic landscapes needs to be viewed.

■ ■ ■

References

Barr, C., Bunce, R., Clarke, R., Fuller, R., Furse, M., Gillespie, M., Hallman, M., Howard, D. and Ness, M. (1993) *Countryside Survey 1990, Main Report*, London: Department of the Environment.

Cheshire, P. (1985) 'The environmental implications of European agricultural support', in D. Baldock and D. Conder (eds) *Can the CAP Fit the Environment? Proceedings of a Seminar*, London: IEEP, CPRE, WWF, 9–18.

Countryside Commission (1989) *Incentives for a New Direction in Farming*, CCP262, Cheltenham: Countryside Commission.

Countryside Council for Wales (1992) *Tir Cymen: a farmland stewardship scheme*, Bangor: Countryside Council for Wales.

Felton, M. (1993) 'Achieving nature conservation objectives: problems and opportunities with economics', *Journal of Environmental Planning and Management* 36(1): 23–31.

Nature Conservancy Council (1977) *Nature Conservation and Agriculture*, London: NCC.

Potter, C. (1998) *Against the Grain: Agri-Environmental Reform in the United States and the European Union*, Wallingford: CAB International.

Scott, Lord Justice (1942) *Report of Committee on Land Utilisation in Rural Areas*, Cmd 6378, London: HMSO.

Swinbank, A. (1996) 'Capping the CAP? Implementation of the Uruguay Round Agreement by the European Union', *Food Policy*, 21(4/5): 393–407.

Westmacott, R. and Worthington, T. (1974) *New Agricultural Landscapes*. Report of a study undertaken during 1972 on behalf of the Countryside Commission, Cheltenham: Countryside Commission.

Chapter 2

CONSIDERING SIGNIFICANCE IN THE LANDSCAPE: DEVELOPING PRIORITIES THROUGH CONSERVATION PLANNING

David Thackray

Rural landscapes are places of enormous variety, depth and sensitivity. They are places where people live, work or take recreation. They can be places of great natural beauty or design, important for their ecology and habitats, their archaeological features, history and historical associations and vernacular buildings. One or all of these attributes may be important, and need to be considered together with any related issues. All need to be understood in order to assess their relative significance, to develop conservation policies, to establish priorities and to achieve their careful management.

Yet this great range of potential values inherent in landscapes can be constraining. Even amongst bodies concerned with conservation there may be tensions, in particular between those concerned with the natural and those whose interest lies with the cultural environment. The constraints derived, for example, from single perceptions can inhibit understanding and can skew judgements. Many disciplines claim landscapes as their special preserve, yet landscapes are physical, social, political and mental constructs allowing the widest possible involvement in their use, meaning and management. Everybody understands the landscape in a different way. With this in mind therefore, we need an approach to the understanding of landscape that can help those with particular responsibilities for a place, to understand its special and various characteristics, determine priorities and achieve a balanced judgement.

Many models have been developed to address this need by the many organisations and agencies concerned with landscape preservation. These range from the structured approaches to landscape assessment on a broad scale developed by the Countryside

Commission (Countryside Commission 1993) and the Countryside Commission for Scotland (Swanwick 1991) to the work by The National Trust on Whole Farm Plans (Young, Jarman and Beddows 1996). This paper will examine some of these approaches and, in particular, the model based on the principles developed in the Australian ICOMOS *Burra Charter* adopted in 1980 (Marquis-Kyle and Walker 1996), and to its special interpretation and methodology in the seminal work by James Semple Kerr, *The Conservation Plan*, first published in 1982 (Semple Kerr 1996). The approaches described in these documents provide a clear rationale for the development of conservation policies for places of cultural significance, but are readily adaptable to cover environmental and ecological or other concerns or attributes of the landscape.

In brief, the process of developing Conservation Plans involves an assessment of what is important or significant about a place; it must be comprehensive in its overview and based on a reasonable level of understanding. It is a technique that is appropriate for single sites and monuments, but it is especially applicable to wider cultural landscapes, wherein many values are encapsulated and where managers have to establish priorities. It will need to consider the statutory and other designations that apply, address the sensitivity and vulnerability of the place to change and consider any issues affecting it, either current or anticipated. The importance of environmental, social and political issues will mean that it has to be seen in its widest contexts. From this understanding a hierarchy of values can be built up. This, in turn, will inform a statement of significance, and a philosophy or a vision for the place for the future. It needs to be periodically reviewed and flexible enough to reflect new and increasing understanding and new values in the future, but should not change substantially in spirit or meaning. Conservation policies flow from this, and should ensure that the significance is managed and retained in the use and development of the place. Management strategies will derive from and respect the underlying conservation principles and, as practical work programmes are completed or as they evolve, will regularly need to refer back, to monitor actions and to protect the spirit of the place.

At the heart of a conservation philosophy lies understanding. So, the assessment of significance is the process of developing understanding, involving consultation and debate to determine what is important to the individuals and communities concerned with the place, and survey and research where broader scientific or technical information is required. It is a process of determining what is important, and to whom, whether it be historic, aesthetic, scientific or social, international, national, regional or local value.

In many instances much of this information already exists and may be well known, so the role of the assessor may be one of collating information, rather than initiating new research. This can be equally true of aesthetic or other qualitative or associative values as it is of values relating to the physical form and fabric. An understanding of the quality of a place is inherent in many landscape designations, such as National Parks and Areas of Outstanding Natural Beauty. Yet these tacit understandings may not be adequate to establish detailed conservation priorities in a developing political climate where there is increasing competition between the reasonable needs for development and those of conservation. Indeed, there may equally be competition between conservation interests for the limited resources that can be applied to an area as values evolve and expectations increase (Sales 1997).

This changing climate of concern about the holistic requirements of landscape conservation is reflected at both international and national levels. Internationally, it is closely reflected in the debate about cultural landscapes, which has seen recognition of their wider value and meaning following intensive debate by the UNESCO World Heritage Committee culminating at an expert meeting at La Petite Pierre in France in 1992. Definitions were drawn up and were subsequently adopted by the World Heritage Committee in Santa Fe, USA, in 1992 as 'Revisions of the Operating Guidelines' for World Heritage Sites (Rossler 1995). These definitions themselves reflect the 'interactions between people and their natural environment over space and time' (Plachter and Rossler 1995, see also Feilden and Jokhileto 1993).

At the other end of the spectrum, the local level, the various initiatives developed and promoted by Common Ground to stimulate concern for 'local distinctiveness' have been taken up by many communities or parishes through schemes such as 'The Parish Map Project'. Through these there has been an increasing realisation of the importance of local conservation (King and Clifford 1985). This is also seen in the increase in local involvement through Local Agenda 21 forums established by most, if not all, Local Authorities following the United Nations Conference on Environment and Development at Rio de Janeiro in 1992 (Quarrie 1992 and see Cullingworth and Nadin 1997: 165–6). Through these Local Agenda 21 activities, there has been a strengthening involvement of local people in issues of environmental, planning, conservation and cultural concern, and the development of a growing realisation of the importance of sustainable development (English Heritage, English Nature, Countryside Commission 1996).

In Britain these changes towards a more holistic and sustainable approach to conservation are also becoming increasingly apparent in the work of agencies such as English Heritage (Fairclough 1995; English Heritage 1997) the Countryside Commission (Countryside Commission 1993) and English Nature (English Nature 1992). They are also reflected in the increasingly diverse surveys of aspects of the landscape being undertaken by organisations such as National Parks, Local Authorities, The National Trust and The National Trust for Scotland, and as part of the Countryside Stewardship Scheme requirements by private and public landowners for the Ministry of Agriculture. Such surveys might include all or some of an extensive range of studies, including biological and ecological surveys, park and garden surveys, archaeological and historic landscape surveys, land-use surveys and historic buildings surveys. These are all designed to increase understanding and to inform conservation management.

From an historic environment perspective this increasing trend towards a broadening understanding of landscapes can be illustrated by examining the changing approach to specialist archaeological and historic landscape surveys. These have been undertaken for many years, to inform requirements for Scheduling, Listing and other designations, and as part of the former county inventory programmes by the Royal Commissions on Historical Monuments. They originally focused on individual archaeological sites and were used in the 1970s and 1980s to enhance the growing county Sites and Monuments Records as an increasingly valuable constraint tool in land-use planning. Now, however, such surveys are commissioned and undertaken where there is a need for more detailed understanding of the historic landscape character of an area, and they frequently adopt a much wider landscape framework. These surveys provide the context for the historic landscape components, including *inter alia* archaeological sites and structures, buildings, boundaries and routeways. They help develop an understanding of the way such features articulate with each other, both spatially and chronologically. Surveys may well be supported by new archaeological research and assessment, involving perhaps evaluation excavations or geophysical survey, and include local historical research to develop a picture of the land-use history of the place. This is important because it is able to demonstrate historic processes affecting an area, involving both change and continuity, and is able to provide historic associations and meanings for even the most ordinary of features. In this way we can understand what happened and how disparate people were involved with and responsible for the building of the character of the place. We can begin to understand, for example, the hardships endured by the small farmer in the eighteenth century dispossessed by enclosure or imparking and driven from the land, as well as the benefits from the same processes received by the large landowner. These sorts of understandings are important because we are often inclined to concentrate resources on the special attributes of a place and ignore the common or ubiquitous features that are a main contributor to landscape character. It is, so often, these minor features, the lanes between fields linking farm to farm, or the old orchard, that are still important to local people and to visitors. This is not to create too bucolic a picture, but to emphasise the importance of the ordinary as well as the exceptional (Clifford and King 1993).

Similarly, the approach being developed for archaeological surveys is also increasingly used for the study of vernacular and other historic buildings, for example Denyer's work in the Lake District relating the buildings and structures to the processes of settlement, agriculture and industry in the landscape (Denyer 1991). Vernacular quality relates to landscape character, and such surveys have also demonstrated that many of our hitherto poorly understood small buildings, cottages, village and farm buildings are actually of great historical as well as landscape significance. Many more than we expected retain medieval features, for example. We can now more confidently ascribe significance to these structures as part of the overall fabric of the place.

So, in building up an understanding of the character of a place, in assessing its significance, we are acquiring knowledge about its physical characteristics, its landform, habitats and ecology and the history and archaeology of its components, the traditions associated with them and the processes they represent. We are also developing an understanding of its aesthetic, symbolic and spiritual qualities and traditions and of its associations with people or events in history that might add to its particular significance. The process of assessment of significance cannot include only historic, cultural or ecological attributes. Places have meanings now for communities, for those who live and work there, for those who use the rural landscape for recreational activities, and for those who administer it.

The Conservation Plan process must also address the contemporary issues that may relate to the place, and consider them in the context of its vulnerability or sensitivity to change. The political framework, planning background, statutory and other designations which apply to a place, the condition of its fabric, economic and environmental issues affecting it, educational values, present meanings and future proposals which might affect its development, all need to be examined and understood. Individual agencies, Local Authorities and conservation bodies are increasingly recognising that, in addressing the conservation of the rural landscape, they cannot confine their concerns to their specific areas of interest alone. They must be alert to wider, even global influences, and they cannot achieve their aims simply by resisting development or exploitation only over the land over which they have statutory or other curatorial responsibilities. They must work with local communities and others, all of whom have an increasing expectation and a right to participate in debates about protecting places where they live or work or visit. This both serves to sustain local distinctiveness, and is part of a wider societal negotiation between conservation and economic development. A 'Statement of Environmental Principles' developed by the National Trust (Thackray, Jarman and Burgon 1995; Jarman 1995) is relevant to all with responsibility towards the rural landscape, who must recognise that these responsibilities include the need to protect their own long-term interests from avoidable environmental change, to protect the wider environment and to ensure that their own activities do not generate adverse environmental impacts. These are issues that need to be considered within the Conservation Plan.

The Conservation Plan should provide the benchmark against which proposals for change can be assessed. The impacts of developments, increases in tourism, changes in agricultural practice and in politics all need to be measured against the Plan, and adjusted to respect the conservation vision, so that it is both achievable and sustainable. It is this full body of evidence which contributes to the understanding of the landscape, and which allows managers to formulate a hierarchy of values, establish priorities and decide the relative significance of a place. It is, therefore, important that these plans should develop principles for long-term management, should avoid being unduly prescriptive and should retain a degree of flexibility in order to accommodate future changes of emphasis without compromising the vision. They need to establish planning and management priorities so that resources can be targeted effectively, for example through Whole Farm Plans, considering in particular, principal land uses such as agriculture, forestry, access and recreation, and landscape conservation and enhancement.

Just as there is a great deal of similarity between the Conservation Plan process and that of Landscape Assessment, which both provide a multi-disciplinary overview and analysis of the character of the landscape, establish significance and inform management planning, so there is also similarity with the use of Whole Farm Plans. These are being developed and used increasingly within, for example, the National Trust and other land-owning conservation bodies, and are being promulgated by the Ministry of Agriculture and associated organisations such as the Farming and Wildlife Advisory Groups. It is self-evident now that farming practice is a major influence on environmental conservation, and there is a growing desire to influence and control day-to-day farming operations. However, conservation must also respect livelihoods. Whole Farm Plans are an aid to the integration of farming, conservation and access on farms, as well as a method of improving environmental practices. Just as with the Conservation Plan process, Whole Farm Plans employ consultation, survey and research and aim to balance the interests of farming with the landscape and conservation concerns. Where necessary, the assessment will highlight the need for more detailed plans to be drawn up, for example where there are features of exceptional conservation value, significant environmental concerns, or where major capital investment is required. Although it is applicable at any stage in farm management, it is of particular value where major changes of farming practice become a possibility, or where social issues relating to the maintenance and support of viable rural communities need to be addressed.

So, having carried out the assessments and evaluations, having drafted the Conservation Plan statement of significance, considered the relevant issues and developed the conservation policies or objectives for the place, operational or management strategies are needed. These equate with the management plan showing how the policy will be implemented and relating to the management structure for achieving these practical aims. They may well comprise a rolling work programme, or could include actions for acquiring resources, for example though an application for Lottery funds. This programme of implementation will be the responsibility of the managers of the place, who have had to undertake the interdisciplinary juggling to determine the work priorities and programmes. Here the responsibility is reasonably clear, although implementation of a management strategy may well involve groups of specialists. However, the achievement of the Conservation Plan itself will certainly be interdisciplinary, the conclusions of a consultative process in which all interested parties should participate, and to which all should be prepared to sign up. The specialisms involved will be as various as the areas of interest and will represent local and national, scientific and technical or purely subjective concerns about the place. The conclusions and synthesis which make up the Conservation Plan can be as short as a side of A4 or a detailed management strategy relating to all the features of significance.

In conclusion, at the heart of this thinking are the places being considered. These are all places that have values and significance, both in themselves and in their wider context. Their diversity, both of habitat and species and of the accumulating stock of cultural heritage, implies scientific values capable of being enhanced by research and deepening understanding, as well as perceptual and other values, such as spiritual values and meanings to residents, neighbours and the wider community. They have value too for public enjoyment, recreation and education. Inherent within the Conservation Plan and its philosophy of conservation is the expectation that what we value today we can share with future participants in future generations. This reflects the dynamics of ongoing processes and sensitive development respecting the spirit of the place. In promoting our aims we need to encourage people's confidence in this dynamism, need to be forward looking with an understanding of the significance of the place and its special qualities, to increase respect for it and to ensure that it is not swamped by the tide of development, political or cultural uniformity or neglect.

■ ■ ■

References

Berry, A. and Brown, I. (eds) (1995) *Managing Ancient Monuments: An Integrated Approach*, Mold: Clwyd Archaeological Service in association with Association of County Archaeology Officers.

Clifford, S. and King, A. (eds) (1993) *Local Distinctiveness: Place, Particularity and Identity*, essays for a conference 28 September, 1993, London: Common Ground.

Countryside Commission (1993) *Landscape Assessment Guidance*, CCP423, Cheltenham: Countryside Commission.

—— (1996) *Views From the Past – Historic Landscape Character in the English Countryside*, CC Working Paper No. 4, Cheltenham: Countryside Commission.

Cullingworth, J.B. and Nadin, V. (1997) *Town and Country Planning in the UK* (12th edition), London: Routledge.

Denyer, S. (1991) *Traditional Buildings and Life in the Lake District*, London: Victor Gollancz Ltd/Peter Crawley in association with National Trust.

English Heritage (1997) *Sustaining the historic environment: new perspectives on the future*, London: English Heritage.

English Heritage, English Nature, Countryside Commission (1996) *Ideas into Action for Local Agenda 21*, Cheltenham: Countryside Commission.

English Nature (1992) *Strategic Planning and Sustainable Development*, an informal consultation paper based on work for English Nature by David Tyldesley Associates in consultation with CAG Management Consultants, Peterborough: English Nature.

Fairclough, G. (1995) 'The Sum of all its Parts: An Overview of the Politics of Integrated Management in England' in Berry and Brown (1995), 17–28.

Feilden, B. and Jokhileto, J. (1993) *Management Guidelines for World Cultural Heritage Sites*, Rome: ICCROM, UNESCO, ICOMOS.

Jarman, R. (1995) 'National Trust – Environmental Principles', *VIEWS* 23.

King, A. and Clifford, S. (1985) *Holding Your Ground*, Aldershot: Common Ground.

Marquis-Kyle, P. and Walker, M. (1996) *The Illustrated Burra Charter*, Brisbane: Australia ICOMOS.

Plachter, H. and Rossler, M. (1995) 'Cultural Landscapes: Reconnecting Culture and Nature' in Von Droste, Plachter and Rossler (1995).

Quarrie, J. (ed.) (1992) *Earth Summit '92: The United Nations Conference on Environment and Development Rio de Janeiro 1992*, London: The Regency Press.

Rossler, M. (1995) 'UNESCO and Cultural Landscape Protection' in Von Droste, Plachter and Rossler (1995).

Sales, J. (1997) 'Achievable Vision', National Trust Estates Department unpublished paper for its National Strategic Plan.

Semple Kerr, J. (1996) *The Conservation Plan*, Sydney: National Trust of Australia (NSW).

Swanwick, C. (1991) *Landscape Assessment Principles and Practice, A Report by Land Use Consultants to the Countryside Commission for Scotland*, London: Land Use Consultants for the Countryside Commission for Scotland.

Thackray, D., Jarman, R. and Burgon, J. (1995) 'The National Trust's approach to integrated conservation management' in Berry and Brown (1995).

Von Droste, B., Plachter, H. and Rossler, M. (1995) *Cultural Landscapes of Universal Value: Components of a Global Strategy*, Jena: G. Fischer in cooperation with UNESCO.

Young, J. Jarman, R. and Beddows, A. (1996) Farm Assessments and Whole Farm Plans, National Trust Internal Guidance Note, Cirencester: National Trust.

Chapter 3

Faⅰrclough

PROTECTING THE CULTURAL LANDSCAPE:
NATIONAL DESIGNATION AND
LOCAL CHARACTER

Graham Fairclough

The rural idyll

The English countryside – by which I mean its historic landscape, its archaeological dimension, its wildlife and pattern of land use, and the 'traditional' and not-so-traditional methods by which it is used and worked – is managed in as many different ways as its character can be described.

In the first place, it is managed as farmland of one sort or another and for related economic uses such as forestry. It is also the home to quarrying, primary industry, manufacturing and, increasingly, activities of other types which could just as easily be in towns and cities but which find the countryside more congenial. All these contribute to the appearance of the countryside. It can probably still be argued that agriculture has the biggest impact, but it is an impact which is changing drastically. It is no longer necessarily the farmer, or even the landlord, who determines what crops or stock are produced, or in what way. These decisions, directly or indirectly, are taken by larger-scale economic and political forces.

The second major influence on the countryside is the Local Authority planning process, allied in a few areas to National Park (and to a much lesser extent, AONB) legislation, and guided now by PPG7 (*The Countryside – Environmental Quality and Economic and Social Development*) and the attitudes and aspirations of the 1995 Rural White Paper (Department of the Environment/MAFF 1995) (see Dormor, this volume). Dire warnings about future loss of green land abound, and may well be justified, but it is probably true to say that without the 1947 Planning Act the countryside would be a much less well-preserved place, and one with less historic character or ecological value. In some parts of the country, the Green Belt has probably been the most powerful force for protecting the countryside from development, constraining our major cities from completely unfettered growth into the countryside. More widely, structure and local development plans and development control have influenced change. On some fronts, other aspects of central government policy have undermined the influence of the planning process (its roads policy, for example, and perhaps in future the effect of centrally imposed house-building targets), but on the whole the planning process has proved its worth. During the 1980s its application to archaeological sites was greatly strengthened, partly by the building up of archaeological expertise in county councils, but particularly at the end of the 1980s by the codification of best practice in PPG16.

Finally, and the main subject of this chapter, a further field of influence comes from various protective designations (Coupe and Fairclough 1991). Setting aside National Parks and AONBs, mentioned above, these designations include protection for archaeological sites (scheduled monuments), architecture (listed buildings), nature conservation (Sites of Special Scientific Interest, supported more recently by various international designations such as Ramsar or SPA), designed landscape (Register of Parks and Gardens), battlefields (the English Heritage non-statutory register), villages and small towns (conservation areas, largely subsumed within the planning process), and hedges (the 1997 Regulations). All these designations are more or less effective tools to protect individual sites, first by marking them as important, fragile and in need of careful management, and second by preventing, or suitably modifying, proposals for damaging activity. Some of them are or can be very extensive areas, but mainly they are relatively small-scale and tightly circumscribed. One or more designations may overlap on a single piece of land (scheduled monuments within SSSIs, for example) but in general the existence of separate legislation and diverse aims and methods conspire to fragment the landscape, separating one component from another on the grounds of narrow definition and different, sometimes competing, interests. They also fragment the landscape by dividing it up into small parcels, which cumulatively cover a tiny proportion of the land area of England. An estimate of the area included in the current Schedule of about 17,000 monuments is only about 20,000 hectares; there are, broadly, 13 million hectares in England. They are also selective (even when they cover a large area) in what they protect, usually taking only the very best, or a representative sample of some sort. Large-scale scheduling of prehistoric remains on moorland, for example, generally excludes the current pattern of hedges and walls, which are not part of the 'monument' and are still in use. The landscape as a whole is virtually unprotected by designation, though it is hard to see how this could sensibly be otherwise. Where 'landscape' designations do exist – AONB for example – they cover such large areas that in many ways they are simply marks of appreciation, not techniques of protection. Usually too they are drawn up to reflect a particular view of landscape (the aesthetic of so-called 'natural beauty' in the case of AONBs) which often neglects and excludes historic landscape, and their influence is partial.

Such widespread designations strengthen the planning process, and buttress specialist designations such as scheduling, but they do not provide truly holistic management of the landscape.

To these three main influences on the countryside – economic and agricultural, public policy such as planning, and statutory designations – needs to be added a fourth issue, that of public use and enjoyment: in other words, access and tourism, including questions of ownership in the widest, cultural sense of the word. This is more a question of use than of influence, but it is significant in terms of its current and potential impact and is the main key to unlocking some of the wider political questions of what society as a whole wishes to do with the countryside.

Nature, culture or heritage?

It is worth recalling that one of the underlying pieces of law about conserving the countryside – the 1968 Countryside Act – imposed a duty to have regard to the desirability of conserving the countryside, not just on the Countryside Commission, but on all government and public bodies including local authorities. However, it did so only in terms of 'natural beauty' and amenity. The same terms support National Park and AONB legislation. It was only in the 1993 Environment Act, in relation to restated powers of National Park Authorities, that the term cultural heritage was added to natural beauty. In general then, the historic environment has to argue its case strongly to be sure of any consideration in AONB or National Park practice. The National Parks all now have at least one archaeological officer, but in some this is a relatively recent step forward.

Current legislation, therefore, does little to emphasise the archaeological, historical or cultural basis of concepts such as natural beauty or landscape. Where legislation attempts to cover all facets of the countryside (for example in the privatisation legislation for the water and electricity industries, which place duties of conservation on the new private utilities), it normally does so in terms of separate provision for landscape (otherwise known as natural beauty and amenity), for nature conservation, and for archaeology and history (the respective responsibilities, in England, of the Countryside Commission, English Nature and English Heritage). Even the most recent legislation (the Hedgerow Regulations 1997) tends to follow this approach with its distinct sets of criteria for importance based on historic, ecological and amenity attributes. PPG7, whilst purporting to give planning guidance on the whole countryside, is disappointing in its recognition of the countryside's historic roots, and of the need to protect historic landscape character. Even more disappointing in this respect was the Rural White Paper (Department of the Environment/MAFF 1995), which scarcely noticed the historic environment.

In practice, however, those who implement the various legislative measures do so increasingly from a position of accepting the ultimate unity of the three interests (Fairclough 1995). At the most strategic level, the three national agencies have produced joint guidance for local planning authorities on conservation issues as a whole (English Heritage, Countryside Commission and English Nature 1993), and have collaborated on the Countryside Character Map and similar initiatives (Countryside Commission 1993; Countryside Commission and English Nature 1996; Fairclough *et al.* 1996). The Countryside Commission in particular has published guidance that makes it clear that landscape character must be seen as a product of history. Beyond government circles, the non-governmental agencies (such as the Council for the Protection of Rural England, Council for British Archaeology and Royal Society for the Protection of Birds) forge alliances through the Countryside and Wildlife Link which similarly promote coordinate approaches.

This integration, however, is almost non-existent at the level of designations and their operation. This is particularly true of designations for archaeological sites and nature conservation sites, which have completely different legal approaches. The main thing they share is a dependence upon top-down, nationally-led identification of the most special sites based on criteria which focus on the scientific and academic value of small sites. They overlook both the more local importance of sites, and the connection between sites and their surroundings. In nature conservation terms this leads to protection of habitats by SSSI designation, for example, which in the long term are probably inadequate to sustain many species of wildlife, and too small on their own to preserve the overall character of the countryside. English Nature's Natural Areas project (see Cooke, this volume) is an important attempt to address the management of the remainder of the natural world between or beyond SSSI enclaves.

Much the same is true of the most effective methods of protecting or managing archaeological sites in the countryside. Both scheduling (and its controls) and the PPG16 planning process are very good tools for examining individual proposals to change sites and for dealing with damaging development. They do not, however, offer the means to manage the character of the whole countryside. In the next section, therefore, scheduling and its effects are offered as an example of how all specialised designations work in the countryside.

Monuments to the past

The 1979 Ancient Monuments and Archaeological Areas Act (the primary *archaeological* legislation) creates controls (Scheduled Monument Consent or SMC) over a very wide, almost comprehensive range of activities within the area of a scheduled monument. 'Works' which require the Secretary of State's approval include repair and alteration, tipping on or burying the site, additions to it, or removal from it, or its demolition, destruction or damage. In practice, virtually anything which disturbs the ground, or scheduled structures above it, requires SMC. There are a few exceptions – removal of archaeological artefacts from ploughsoil, for example – but the range of work controlled is very wide, certainly wider than listed building controls (with their exclusions for repair and inadequate definition of the crucial word 'demolition'), SSSI (generally restricted to controlling specified damaging operations) and planning permissions (limited to a legally-defined concept of development which excludes, for example, agriculture).

This breadth of coverage is reflected in the manner in which SMC controls are operated by English Heritage and the Secretary of State. SMC is based on an underlying presumption of refusing consent for work which adversely affects a scheduled monument's form, appearance, archaeological content, integrity, visual amenity and scientific importance. The controls are supported by statutory powers for grant-aid, and by offences of damage and carrying out unauthorised work. There is also control over metal-detecting, geophysical survey and archaeological excavation.

This strong level of protection is however kept within limits by two factors. First, a system of permitted development (called class consents) exempts specified works from the need for applying for SMC. Whilst these works are largely defined in terms of urgency (for instance, health and safety matters) or convenience (for instance, *de minimis* matters like RCHME survey pegs or operational matters like EH activity), they are also defined in terms of precedence. In particular, existing agricultural operations are granted class consent. In practice, therefore, this restricts SMC controls over agriculture to controlling agricultural change or intensification such as the ploughing-up for the first time of pasture containing known archaeological remains. The majority of agricultural operations, because ongoing, are not controlled except through a cumbersome, costly and so far virtually unused procedure of revoking individual class consents. The single largest cause of erosion and disturbance to archaeological sites is therefore not controlled by scheduling.

Apart from this major area, the scheduling regime is perhaps more effective at protecting individual features in the countryside than any other designation. The main contribution to the protection of the Register of Historic Parks and Gardens, for example, is through the planning process, as a carefully flagged-up (in PPG15) material consideration for development control. Conservation Areas, of which a large proportion include villages and rural small towns, sometimes with extensive hinterlands in the surrounding countryside (the so-called 'rural Conservation Areas'), mainly provide protection for the built element of the countryside rather than other 'soft' or living features. The Hedgerows Regulations are too new (and in any event under review) to be assessed, but early signs are that they will prove cumbersome in use, and their criteria may be too tightly defined to offer any significant solution to the issue of hedgerow loss. In any case, the Regulations only prevent removal. They do little to encourage, and nothing to require, the right sort of sympathetic management which is essential to a hedge's preservation. For hedges, therefore, incentive schemes within Countryside Stewardship are likely to continue to be their best defence. For stone field walls, so significant in upland areas, there is at present no protection except slightly implausibly through conservation areas, though some incentives exist in National Parks and ESAs.

Returning to scheduling, the other limit of the regime is to the scale of its application. 'Monument' as defined by law must contain a 'building, structure or work' or its remains. This is a broad definition, but it nevertheless rules out some types of archaeology, such as prehistoric activity sites surviving only as ploughsoil lithic scatters. More significantly for countryside issues, it rules out many types of countryside feature which are the by-products of past human activity: earthwork wood banks may be scheduled, but the coppiced woodland which they enclose is itself generally exempt. Similarly, the bounds of a deerpark might find a place on the Schedule, but not its interior. A larger exclusion, however, is the inapplicability of scheduling to structures or features still in use; whilst legally it might be argued that they are schedulable, the SMC controls are designed for dealing with abandoned monuments where our aim is to preserve them largely unchanged. For features still in use (and hence in need of continuing management) the system simply is not effective, no matter how archaeological in their form or fabric, or how significant they may be in constructing historic landscape character. Scheduling does not protect the countryside itself, therefore, merely some of its components.

There is also the question of defining the extent of a scheduled monument. The SMC controls are rigorous, highly detailed and centralised, and they can only be reasonably applied where they are absolutely necessary. This means that the boundaries of scheduled monuments are always tightly drawn, and exclude the areas between sites which are not close-spaced. Large area schedulings are therefore rare, and restricted to areas of dense archaeology, mainly unenclosed moorland with low levels of modern activity.

Scheduling is also restricted to the most important and best preserved examples of each monument class, and may not be thought appropriate for all of these, depending on the feasibility of their long-term preservation. At the level of historic landscape character, therefore, the archaeological designation system affects only a very small part of the overall picture. Nevertheless, the Schedule, with its associated controls, is a crucially important mechanism for protecting a minority of archaeological sites. Scheduled monuments however can act as 'anchors' of strong and sharply-focused protection to which other types of conservation and management of the surrounding landscape can sometimes be fixed (English Heritage 1997; Thackray, this volume). These other methods must take account of the triple influences of land use, public policy, and designations mentioned at the beginning of this chapter. In particular however they should be based on a much deeper understanding and public awareness of the overall historic character of the landscape, and of its need for continuing and changing management.

Gaps in the hedge

The 1979 Act does not, then, significantly contribute in a direct way to the positive or active management of the wider countryside. It makes provision (in section 17) for voluntary management agreements which in some situations have proved extremely useful in helping farmers and others to carry out erosion repair, enhance the condition of monuments and occasionally change the more damaging of farming regimes. In most cases, however, the efficacy of management agreements is pre-empted, partly by the difficulty of changing the farm management of a very small area, and partly because of the overwhelming pressure of economic and political forces, notably the Common Agriculture Policy (see Potter, this volume). The fact that area-based schemes within the Environmentally Sensitive Area and Countryside Stewardship programmes have greater success demonstrates that the problem of small scale is a major factor in limiting the effectiveness of specialised designations. The image of a scrub-covered barrow fenced off and surrounded by deep-ploughed farmland is emblematic.

In short, change in agricultural management can be achieved if sufficiently large areas are tackled, but it is very difficult to achieve on a small scale. It is however rarely possible to bring large areas into designations designed to be selective and which carry strong controls. In contrast, the limitations of Environmentally Sensitive Areas and Countryside Stewardship show that scale is not all and that the wider context of CAP and politics needs to be dealt with as well. The same is probably true of hedgerow incentives: they may be effective at the margins, where a farmer's decision can be finely balanced, but they are not effective where there are strong economic pressures to maintain environmentally *in*sensitive farming.

In summary, whether in terms of protection against development or of positive management for archaeological features, the existing system is insufficient and inap-propriate. It stands at three removes from a sensible model for an effective form of countryside management. At the first remove, it concerns itself with too small a range of the archaeological countryside; at the second it concerns itself largely with areas which are too precisely defined and thus too small to influence or modify overall landscape utilisation strategies (the ability of the planning process to take setting into account is an exception, as is, perhaps, the scale at which historic parks and gardens or battlefields and a few Scheduled Monuments are defined); at the third it attempts to protect sites for merely one of a wide range of possible reasons, and to do so largely in isolation from, or frequently in opposition to, the most important political pressures on rural life.

This latter point is the most significant. A system of separate specialised desig-nation and protective controls for ancient monuments, buildings, hedgerows, nature reserves, etc. could be made to work extremely well if it was set within a wide enough supportive context. It is straightforward to demonstrate that any particular scheduled monument also has nature conservation value and contributes to land-scape character. The designation system perhaps could therefore, to some extent, be made to work in an integrated way. At present, however, the only integrated context that exists is the planning process, which is limited to considering matters of land use and to controlling development (which is itself so narrowly defined that agriculture, crucially, escapes planning control). Furthermore, the types of value recognised in designations are only some of several which people attach to any given piece of land or feature. This question has come to the fore during the exploration by English Heritage of ideas about sustainable development (English Heritage 1997); for archaeological sites a set of broad values has been defined.

These are, put simply:

- **cultural values**: the historic environment helps to define a sense of place and provides a context for everyday life. Its appreciation and conservation foster distinctiveness at local, regional and national level. It reflects the roots of our society and records its evolution.

- **educational and academic values**: the historic environment is a major source of information about our ancestors, the evolution of their society and the characteristics of past environments. It provides a means for new generations to understand the past and their own culture. We can also use archaeology to learn about the long-term impact (and sustainability or otherwise) of past human activity and development, and to use this knowledge when planning our future.

- **economic values**: the historic environment can make a significant contribution to economic development by encouraging tourism, but more generally it also supports viable communities by creating good environments where people will prefer to live and work.

- **resource values**: longer-lived buildings usually make better use of the energy and resources that were used during their construction, and reuse is usually more economic than demolition and redevelopment. Conservation is inherently sustainable.

- **recreational values**: the historic environment plays a very significant role in providing for people's recreation and enjoyment. Increasingly, the past and its remains in the present are a vital part of people's everyday life and experiences.

- **aesthetic values**: archaeology and historic buildings make a major contribution to the aesthetic quality of townscapes and landscapes, enhancing the familiar scene of our historic towns and villages and giving historic depth and interest to our countryside.

The values in this list (in which only the 'academic' value significantly influences decisions on what to schedule) are mainly those of people for whom the archaeological site has some significance to begin with. For a landowner, other factors (which to some extent are in opposition to its archaeological value) might weigh more heavily – development value, for example, or sale value, mineral value, business potential. Most significantly, both these two lists of values are furthermore but a single column in the full table that would be needed to reflect the real world of land-use decisions. A parallel set can be drawn up for landscape character, one for nature conservation, and of course several for key rural issues such as employment, housing, rural identity and farming. All these ways of valuing land need to be taken into account if the archaeological landscape is to be properly managed. Against this complex backdrop, the struggle to designate and protect a few special sites does not seem very ambitious.

Seeing the wood for the trees – an object lesson

As an example of how difficult it can be to manage the countryside, we can take current government policy, set out in the 1995 Rural White Paper (Department of the Environment/MAFF 1995) to double woodland cover over the next half century, so that it reaches about 15 per cent of total land area, as it was last in 1086. In origin, this desire arises from a belief that woodland is intrinsically environmentally beneficial, that England has a much lower ('too' low, by some mystical calculation) proportion of woodland than other European countries, that more woodland is necessary to ensure that some types of wildlife population can be increased, and that it will make the landscape more attractive. To someone from an archaeological background, most of these reasons are spurious. There should be a general suspicion of any attempt to turn back the clock, and to recreate a past landscape which existed (perhaps) in quite specific circumstances. Yet the 'Domesday level of woodland cover' is held up by some as a goal for tree-planting, providing yet another example of the popular nostalgia for non-existent golden ages. Is a Domesday level of woodland sustainable with twentieth-century levels of population and land pressure, or is it proposed to lower those two as well?

There is also anxiety that the historic landscape, which has been created as a result of long-term woodland clearance and management and which has its own valuable character, will be destroyed. The character of the landscape in Midland England is purely the result of over a thousand years of farming which has deliberately replaced woodland with farmland, first open-field arable and more latterly Enclosure field patterns. A decision to over-plant this with a new mixed landscape of conservation woods that owes nothing to the past is not one to be taken lightly. Elsewhere in England, in the western and eastern provinces of the country, the land is still more heavily wooded, but the woodland is of a particular type, its location and form closely respecting the evolution of the landscape and its land use over millennia; here too the creation of new landscapes dislocated from the past needs very careful thought.

There are no obvious candidates for woodland creation that do not work to the detriment of historic landscape character. A favourite suggestion for locating new woodlands is 'those boring flat bits around Peterborough', but what of those who value the peculiar historic resonance of the Fens, their huge skies and wide vistas, their cold winds and steely calm? These are for some people valued landscapes, for others some of the country's most profitable farmland (for the present). They are also areas which contain buried archaeology of world importance. Large-scale tree-planting might be able to avoid damaging individual archaeological sites, and might actually improve their condition or public amenity value if they are, say, currently under arable; but it might desiccate wetland sites and destroy or, at best, hide from view other sites. In no part of England is it likely that extensive woodland creation will enhance historic landscape character or, for example, help much towards hedgerow preservation. It is not enough to locate new woodland to avoid whichever areas of the landscape are considered to be most historic, because few if any areas have no historic character (Countryside Commission 1996: 2; PPG15 para 6.40).

The intention to increase woodland cover for its own sake – the creation of 'conservation woodland' – raises questions of sustainability. Historically, woodland has been allowed to survive, usually carefully managed, or has been planted, almost only where there have been strong economic and agrarian – and occasionally polit-ical – reasons. In the absence of similar historic processes, will large-scale planting be sustainable in the long term? There is also a risk that some of the present historic landscape will be damaged for the sake of unsustainable woodland which will not survive in the long term. It is arguable perhaps that conservation for its own sake (for example, allied to meeting rising recreational pressure of the countryside) is, or will become, an influential social process sufficiently strong to support a doubling of woodland cover, although there must be doubt that amenity or recreation factors will ever provide a strong enough economic imperative.

In practice, however, it is probable that decisions about creating large-scale conservation woodland will be driven almost wholly by commercial factors. When it comes to selecting land for new woodland, and designing planting schemes, landowners will be reluctant to use the best agricultural land, or land with more lucrative development potential, and the task of fitting new woodland sympathet-ically into the historic landscape – already difficult – is thus compromised from the start. Economically-driven decision-makers, in other words, are likely to see afforestation primarily in a commercial light. The scale of investment required for woodland creation may prohibit it as a conservation-led practice. Market pressures will either render woodland creation uneconomic, or push it into areas (for instance moorland or low-quality agricultural land where archaeology has survived best, and which are often the most valued scenic landscapes) which woodland conservation-ists would not themselves have chosen. The 41 per cent of respondents to a recent Countryside Commission and Forestry Commission consultation who think that woodland planting will enhance landscape and local distinctiveness may be under-estimating the extent to which commercial pressures will be dominant, and over-estimating the influence of landscape architects. The trees could be planted as hedgerows, of course, but it is difficult enough to sustain the current manage-ment of existing hedges in the countryside without adding new ones – the priority for hedges ought to be to maintain the historic ones we already have.

Over a long enough time span, a doubling of England's tree cover might bring economic returns for landowners, but there will be little gain for rural employ-ment or maintenance of rural communities. It is even debatable whether the majority of the public will, in the end, welcome a heavily wooded countryside, especially if market forces dictate conifers for softwood. Extensive woodland is not part of the English sense of identity or of place; in mythology and folklore, it often represents threat rather than stability, alienation rather than belonging, and wild rather than nurtured landscape; almost the antithesis of the perceived character of the English countryside.

This brief digression into the woods has been intended to demonstrate something of the complexity of countryside management, and particularly of the range of interests and viewpoints to be accommodated. A good case can certainly be made for increasing England's woodland cover. My point however is that such a case (which has not yet been properly made) represents only one viewpoint. It is not necessarily an entirely positive proposal. Increased tree-planting began as a conservation-led idea, but it is easy to see it being hijacked by commercial interests just as damaging to the countryside as those supported by the CAP. The pros and cons of returning to Domesday Book levels of woodland are very hard to balance (and the attempt to do so could stretch to breaking point efforts to achieve better integration between archaeological, natural and landscape conservation), but some of the consequences can already be foreseen.

A landscape with figures

The current position therefore is that the existing patchwork of specialised designations may be effective in the protection and good management of certain aspects of the countryside's character, but that it does this in a fragmentary way which leaves many of the fundamentals of the countryside as an entity largely untouched. Archaeological designations are obliged to focus on tightly-defined individual monuments, with insufficient concern for setting, inter-connections and overall context. The listing system has difficulty in dealing at the lower end of the architectural spectrum with the more commonplace buildings which comprise the bulk of the countryside's built heritage. Nature conservation designations protect the most important habitats, but not the wider hinterland which they often need for their long-term support. For amenity landscape, National Parks or Areas of Outstanding Natural Beauty provide a high level of care, but only cover part of the country.

There is a lack of comprehensive attention to the question of overall character as opposed to particular sites and a lack (still) of integration between the different specialised conservation interests. Most of all, however, there is a lack of real engagement between conservation and environmentalists on the one side, and the concerns of those who live or work in the countryside on the other. The message that an appropriately protected and nurtured countryside offers the best chance for rural economic health and social vitality, despite much championing by the Countryside Commission, has not been taken up widely enough. Nor yet has the opposite message – that our use of the countryside will not in the long term be sustainable without taking full account of its environmental health and, in cultural and historic terms, its character. Rural employment no longer has to be agricultural. It is not an empty cliché to say that business companies which create employment are drawn to rural areas because of issues such as quality of life, ecological interest and historic interest – in other words because of countryside and landscape character. If this is not protected, 'new' employment will not be drawn in.

This is why English Heritage has been beginning to move in two new directions – a more broadly-based assessment of the whole countryside which does not include designation and legal protection, under the term historic landscape or historic character, and the adoption of the metaphors and ambitions of sustainable development. Understanding why the landscape looks like it does – and more importantly (because it explains how we might keep it in good shape) how it was made by generations of human activity – does not mean that every detail must be protected. It does mean however that we can set levels for change (in different parts of the country, for different types of activity or development, or for conservation attributes) which allow overall character to be maintained or, if desired, altered as long as we are aware of the consequences. Identifying special sites – and protecting them by legal designation – will need to form part of this approach, but only for key sites. The designations we have cannot be extended indefinitely to cover broader and broader categories or larger and larger areas. To do so risks destroying the effectiveness of the whole designation system, whilst still never getting to the root of the problem – which is to encourage and achieve better care for all elements of the countryside, including the commonplace as well as the most important.

We are already seeing this shift towards the commonplace in several areas. Pioneering work on local distinctiveness by Common Ground (a small but energetic and imaginative organisation that works to encourage people to value and enjoy their own familiar surroundings, regardless of whether they are rare, unusual or important) was of course ground-breaking in emphasising the importance of place to people, and the value of the commonplace. It has been followed up by, for example, aspects of Countryside Stewardship and the production by local authorities in partnership with the wider community of *Local Agenda 21*, designed to establish what is valued about an area and to define agreed frameworks for future planning and development (English Heritage, Countryside Commission and English Nature 1996). Even Government guidance recognises the point – PPG16 emphasises that sites of 'more local' significance are material considerations in planning decisions. The Conservation Area concept (originating in the Civic Amenities Act 1967) was an early attempt to get behind individual buildings to the character of the whole settlement – the 'cherished and familiar scene'. It is currently being given a new lease of life in the promotion by English Heritage of Conservation Area Approaches and by the Countryside Commission of Village Design Statements. English Heritage's Monuments Protection Programme, often associated only with scheduling, is in fact a thematic review of all archaeological sites. It provides a much needed depth of assessment including local as well as national importance

(English Heritage 1996). Finally, English Heritage's development of robust (and rapid) Historic Landscape Assessments in partnership with local government in, for example, Cornwall, Avon, Derbyshire and Gloucestershire has provided a new way of characterising and recognising the countryside's historic depth. Parallel work at national level includes the mapping for English Heritage of settlement and field diversity, as well as the better known Countryside Character Map described by Robert Cooke in Chapter 10 of this book. All these initiatives, whether at national or local level, are dedicated towards increasing understanding of the diversity and sensitivity of the countryside with a view to guiding its future management and evolution comprehensively, not just in pockets of conservation-designated land.

■   ■   ■

References

Countryside Commission (1993) *Landscape Assessment Guidance*, CCP 423, Cheltenham: Countryside Commission.
—— (1996) *Views From the Past – Historic Landscape Character in the English Countryside*, CCWP4, Cheltenham: Countryside Commission.
Countryside Commission and English Nature (1996) *The Character of England: landscape wildlife and natural features*, CCX41, Cheltenham: Countryside Commission.
Coupe, M. and Fairclough, G.J. (1991) 'Protection for the historic and natural landscape' *Landscape Design* 201: 24–30.
Department of the Environment/Ministry of Agriculture, Fisheries and Food (1995) *Rural England: a nation committed to a living countryside*, Cm 3016, London: HMSO.
Department of the Environment, Transport and the Regions (1994) *Planning Policy Guidance Note 15: Planning and the Historic Environment*, London: The Stationery Office.
—— (1997) *Planning Policy Guidance Note 7: the Countryside – Environmental Quality and Economic and Social Development*, London: The Stationery Office.
English Heritage (1996) *The Monuments Protection Programme 1986–96 in retrospect*, London: English Heritage.
—— (1997) *Sustaining the Historic Environment: new perspectives on the future*, London: English Heritage.
English Heritage, Countryside Commission and English Nature (1993) *Conservation Issues in Local Plans*, CCP 420, Cheltenham: Countryside Commission.
—— (1996) *Ideas into action for Local Agenda 21*, CCX 37, Cheltenham: Countryside Commission with English Heritage and English Nature.
Fairclough, G.J. (1995) 'The Sum of all its Parts: An Overview of the Politics of Integrated Management in England', in A.Q. Berry and I.W. Brown (eds) *Managing Ancient Monuments – an Integrated Approach*, Mold: Clwyd Archaeological Service in association with Association of County Archaeology Officers, 17–28.
Fairclough, G., Lambrick, G. and McNab, A. (eds) (1996) *Yesterday's World, Tomorrow's Landscape: the English Heritage Historic Landscape Project*, London: English Heritage.

PART TWO

Mechanisms and Instruments

Chapter 4

CURRENT PLANNING POLICIES AND LEGISLATION FOR HISTORIC RURAL LANDSCAPES

Ian Dormor

Introduction

This chapter provides an overview of the management of the rural historic landscape under current town and country planning policies and legislation. It provides some historical background to countryside planning together with a consideration of the pressures which impact upon rural historic landscapes and the mechanisms which exist to mitigate their effects. Conservation of the historic environment, in the context of today's philosophy of sustainability, raises questions which go to the core of resource management in the dynamic environment that is the countryside. New approaches to the identification and quantification of archaeological resources have appeared and are developing rapidly.

An enormous amount of England's archaeological capital has been squandered in the past as a result of misplaced agricultural policies and a reluctance to implement land-use legislation, but over the past decade there has been a marked appreciation that the historic environment is a finite and fragile resource whose existence is fundamental to the appearance and character of the countryside. Historic rural landscapes are, after all, the result of man's interaction with the environment over millennia.

Archaeology and planning

The archaeological resource, whether in terms of discrete sites or entire landscapes, shares a working environment with agriculture and forestry, two industries which are fundamental to the appearance and management of the contemporary landscape and, critically, largely exempt from normal planning constraints (see 'The General Permitted Development Order' below). This is the very stuff of conflict. The introduction of Planning Policy Guidance note 16 (PPG16), *Archaeology and Planning* (Department of the Environment 1990a) identifies archaeology as a material consideration in the planning process, which must be taken into account *before* the determination of planning applications, thus covering practically every urban eventuality. Furthermore, it has begun to shift the onus of meeting the costs of archaeological investigation and curation from the taxpayer to the developer. In the rural environment, however, where agriculture and forestry lie outside the planning system, PPG16 does not have such blanket applicability. It does cover mineral extraction and all non-agricultural development, but the day-to-day activities of farmers and foresters are largely outside the purview of the Local Planning Authority archaeologist. One might therefore argue that PPG16 is not applicable to 75 per cent of the land surface of England, and the archaeology it contains derives no benefit.

This apparent dichotomy in the planning system between urban and rural contexts has its roots in the enabling legislation. Born in 1947, the Town and Country Planning system has developed, albeit with the tinkering of governments of all political hues, into top-down legislation administered bottom-up by Local Planning Authorities (LPAs). As Potter (this volume) has noted, the philosophy of the 1947 Act was that the principal threat to the countryside was from urban development, and that farming and forestry were benign land uses. This viewpoint permeated the formulation of planning legislation for 50 years and originated in the Scott Committee's Report (Scott 1942), which informed the drafting of the *1947 Town and Country Planning Act*. The Report said: 'Farmers and foresters are the nation's gardeners. The beauty and pattern of the countryside are a direct result of the cultivation of the soil and there is no antagonism between use and beauty'. At its simplest, farming would continue to maintain the appearance of the English countryside and the planning system would control development in the built-up areas.

The naivety of this thinking is profound and yet understandable since the scale and technology of contemporary agriculture were unimaginable in the 1940s, and the propensity for inflicting such rapid change on the landscape was therefore unthinkable. As agriculture and forestry have developed into highly capitalised industries, virtually free of planning encumbrance, there have been calls to impose planning controls over their activities by influential lobby groups such as the Council for the Protection of Rural England (CPRE) and the County Wildlife Trusts. However agriculture is an industry with close links to central government through the Ministry of Agriculture, Fisheries and Food (MAFF) and its practitioners maintain strong cohesion and lobbying powers through the National Farmers Union (NFU) and the Country Landowners' Association (CLA). Through these alliances and the ability to influence policy-making, farming has enjoyed a position of privilege denied to other industries. As a result it has successfully resisted numerous calls to bring its activities under planning control. Rather than impose legislation, all postwar governments have sought the voluntary cooperation of farmers in attempts to exercise a degree of control over their activities.

The General Permitted Development Order

The mechanism by which agriculture and forestry are excluded from planning control is the General Permitted Development Order. Under the Town and Country Planning General Development Order 1988 certain types of development are classified as 'permitted development' and no application for planning permission is necessary. Class VI of the schedule extends exemptions to agriculture as follows:

> *The carrying out on agricultural land having an area of more than 0.4ha and comprised in an agricultural unit of building or engineering operations requisite for the use of the land for the purposes of agriculture (other than the placing on land of structures not designed for those purposes or the provision and alteration of dwellings), so long as:*
>
> *(1) The ground covered by a new building does not exceed 465 square metres. Further, if it is erected within 90 metres of an existing building (other than a dwelling) on the same unit that was erected or in the course of erection in the two preceding years, then the combined floor area of the buildings must not exceed 465 square metres.*
>
> *(2) The height of the building does not exceed 12 metres, or 3 metres if within 3km of the perimeter of an aerodrome.*
>
> *(3) No part of the building or works (other than moveable structures) is within 25 metres of a trunk or classified road.*
>
> *The farmer may also extract minerals without permission provided they are:*
>
> *(1) From land held for the purposes of agriculture.*
>
> *(2) Used for the fertilization of that land (e.g. lime).*
>
> *(3) Used for the maintenance, improvement or alteration of buildings or works on the farm that are used for agricultural purposes (e.g. stone).*
>
> *(4) At least 25 metres from a trunk or classified road.*

Similar exemptions apply for forestry.

Landscape designation

In the absence of direct legislation over rural land use, landscape designation has been employed extensively as a means of conserving the countryside. The *National Parks and Access to the Countryside Act 1949* set up the National Parks Commission, a government body whose remit included the selection and designation of National

Parks, Areas of Outstanding Natural Beauty (AONBs) and Long-Distance Footpaths. By 1955 ten National Parks had been designated (see Smith, this volume). The top tier of landscape designation, the Parks, were areas where:

(a)   the character of the landscape would be strictly preserved,
(b)   access and facilities for public open air enjoyment would be amply provided,
(c)   wildlife and buildings and places of architectural and historic interest would be suitably protected, while
(d)   established farming use would be effectively maintained.

AONBs represented a subsidiary tier of designation for landscape of high quality but with lesser potential for outdoor recreation. Until the introduction of autonomous National Park Authorities on 1 April 1997 all but two of the National Parks were administered by County Council committees. AONBs in contrast have always been a non-statutory component of development plans: areas in which county planning authorities operate special planning policies. Following the Countryside Commission report on planning and management in AONBs (Smart and Anderson 1990) some of the 41 AONBs have acquired management teams with a remit to:

(a)   conserve and enhance natural beauty,
(b)   ensure that the economic and social needs of local communities can be met without compromising natural beauty,
(c)   improve the management of recreation and tourism.

The 1949 National Parks legislation also enabled another government body, the Nature Conservancy (now English Nature) to declare, under Section 19, National Nature Reserves (NNRs) and Sites of Special Scientific Interest (SSSIs). These are sites or tracts of ecologically or geologically important landscape where special management practices are followed in order to conserve habitats for wildlife. NNRs are either owned or controlled by English Nature or held by approved bodies such as wildlife trusts. SSSIs are mainly privately owned or managed. At the beginning of 1997, there were 183 NNRs covering 69,722 hectares and 3,900 SSSIs covering 951,186 hectares. The 1949 Act also enabled local authorities to declare Local Nature Reserves (LNRs) on 'any land in their area' with the agreement of the landowner and the Nature Conservancy.

The designation process has seen recent applications on a European and global scale for conservation of the natural environment. Two examples are the Special Protection Areas (SPAs) declared in accordance with the European Union's Council Directive of 1979 on the Conservation of Wild Birds and Ramsar sites which are wetlands of international importance designated under the Ramsar Convention of 1973 (named after the town in Iran in which it was signed).

In summary, designation is a means of declaring areas defined by lines on maps as 'special' on account of scenic beauty, ecological quality or propensity for quiet enjoyment and countryside recreation. Designation has been widely and successfully applied: currently 50 per cent of the English landscape is covered by a

designation of some sort (Bromley 1990). Some of the more powerful designations, e.g. National Parks, AONBs and NNRs enable some degree of control to be
exercised over potentially harmful land-use practices such as insensitive tree-felling
and afforestation, moorland conversion to improved pasture and the modification
of traditional farm buildings for new uses by means of special planning policies and
management planning (Countryside Commission 1992). Landscape designation is
not without criticism for it has the propensity to create a multi-tiered countryside,
imputing lesser value to excluded areas (Blunden and Curry 1988). Historic landscapes may be particularly vulnerable in this respect, since they are not necessarily
either scenic or of high ecological value and may therefore be overlooked by designation processes. In the absence of national designation for historic landscapes there
is no statutory mechanism for safeguarding them in areas lying outside the National
Parks and other protected landscapes described above.

Planning policy guidance notes

The Town and Country Planning system takes an overview of land use through the
formulation of Development Plans. Local Planning Authorities usually work on a
two-tier system with Structure Plans which address planning strategies at the county
or unitary level, and Local Plans which deal with matters at borough, district or
local level. Government policy is passed down to LPAs via *Planning Policy Guidance
Notes* (PPGs) which address diverse matters ranging from traffic management to
archaeology. They also act as an explanatory link between planning policies and
other policies which influence development and land use. Two PPGs in addition to
PPG16 *Archaeology and Development* (discussed above) have particular pertinence
to the conservation of historic rural landscapes.

PPG15 *Planning and the Historic Environment* (Department of the Environment
1994), although principally directed towards the built environment, acknowledges
that the wider historic rural landscape is dependent upon active land-use practices.
It states that Local Planning Authorities should encompass the entire landscape
rather than focus upon designated areas and that development plans should acknowledge the historic dimension of the landscape (paragraph 2.26). Policies should have
the benefit of adequate baseline data in order that well-informed judgements can
be made (paragraph 2.13).

PPG7 *The Countryside – Environmental Quality and Economic and Social Development*
(Department of the Environment 1997) appeared in February 1997 and is a revi-
sion of the earlier PPG7 entitled *The Countryside and the Rural Economy*. Its wider
remit stems from the White Paper *Rural England: a Nation Committed to a Living
Countryside* (Department of the Environment/MAFF 1995) and, in the main, the
overriding ethos of the PPG is that of sustainable development as defined by
the *Brundtland Report* (World Commission on Environment and Development 1987):
'managing the countryside in ways that meet current needs without compromising

the ability of future generations to meet theirs'. A reflection of a shift away from the planners' obsession to protect agricultural land at all costs is the statement in paragraph 2.18 which says that the best land (Agricultural Land Classification grades 1, 2 and 3a) can be developed if the alternative was a need to develop lower-grade land with an environmental value, recognised by a statutory landscape, wildlife, historic or archaeological designation. It recognises that archaeological and historical features are irreplaceable and that restoration is not an option.

The Ancient Monuments and Archaeological Areas Act 1979

The main legislation for archaeological sites is the *Ancient Monuments and Archaeological Areas Act 1979*. Disappointingly it is focused upon discrete archaeological sites and has no mechanism to protect the wider rural historic landscape. The Act represents a philosophy of monumentality which the Council for British Archaeology (CBA) has criticised for being 'a thinly modernised version of Victorian thinking' (Council for British Archaeology 1993, 4). The legislation is only applicable to Scheduled Ancient Monuments – designated archaeological sites which meet the criteria for 'national importance'. A Scheduled Ancient Monument is in theory safe from cultivation damage and from changes in land management through the mechanism of Scheduled Monument Consent, administered by English Heritage (see Fairclough, this volume, for more detailed discussion). Nevertheless, there are loopholes which render the legislation relatively toothless: for example, existing damaging operations often continue through the mechanism of Class Consents, which detail exemptions from normal Scheduled Monument control. Currently the greater (unscheduled) part of the archaeological resource has no legal protection, being beyond the remit of PPG16, but this situation should improve as a result of the English Heritage Monuments Protection Programme and the Monuments at Risk Survey adding a significant number of new sites to the Schedule of Ancient Monuments.

Countryside management legislation

More broadly-based countryside management legislation increasingly seeks to incorporate some degree of protection for rural archaeology and historic landscapes in the absence of any specific statutes. The influence of the CBA is apparent in the inclusion of archaeology in much diverse legislation which is principally aimed at securing environmental improvements in the countryside where historic landscapes and archaeology are classified as 'amenity'. This can be seen in the *Wildlife and Countryside Act 1981* which enables a degree of protection for historic landscape components through Section 39 management agreements for the conservation and enhancement of a landscape amenity.

The *Countryside Act 1968* remodelled the National Parks Commission into the Countryside Commission, a body charged with a new brief to oversee the entire countryside, rather than just the designated areas. As an organisation at the spearhead of countryside planning policy development, the influence of the Countryside Commission has been substantial. It has been at the forefront of rural policy-making, as the Government's rural adviser, developing new initiatives and approaches to the countryside. Its efforts have also been closely watched and largely supported by the rapidly expanding environmental lobby – so-called 'green' organisations, formed from a myriad of wildlife, conservation, landscape, recreation and special interest groups. An articulate and coordinated lobby, the environmental movement has sought to influence and challenge Westminster over the glaringly undemocratic exclusion of the land-based industries from planning regulation. Concerns such as the removal of hedgerows, the decline of wildlife habitats and biodiversity, and the denial of access rights to the open countryside have been voiced with ever increasing volume.

A manifestation of the influence of the environmental lobby upon MAFF came in 1984 with the Halvergate Marshes controversy. A novel management agreement was offered to dissuade a farmer from ploughing the Halvergate grazing marshes and to reinstate the traditional grazing regime in return for a suite of flat-rate subsidies. British influence upon the Commission of the European Communities resulted in the introduction of a new designation known as Environmentally Sensitive Areas (ESAs) by means of a European Directive (Article 19 of the Structures Regulations). The passing of the *Agriculture Act 1986* gave powers to MAFF to declare Environmentally Sensitive Areas where 'the maintenance or adoption of particular agricultural methods is likely to facilitate the conservation, enhancement or protection of the nature conservation, amenity or archaeological and historic interest of an area' and to provide financial incentives to encourage sensitive farming practices in the ESAs (see McCrone, this volume). Under the scheme 10 per cent of the agricultural land in England is eligible, and take-up currently covers 44 per cent of the eligible area (Department of the Environment/MAFF 1996) (and see Figure 1.1 of this volume).

The *Finance Act 1986* has been particularly useful in securing the long-term management of historic rural landscapes. The Act enables an owner to agree to manage land to a specific set of prescriptions in return for an undertaking that, on his/her death, the Treasury will consider exempting that land from Inheritance Tax. Two examples of where this has been used for the benefit of historic rural landscapes are the Weld Estate in Dorset (Keen and Carreck 1987) and the Bilsdale Estate in North Yorkshire (Statham 1982).

Statutory undertakers' legislation

Recognition of archaeology has also been incorporated in the statutory undertakers' legislation for many years. The actual wording frequently takes the form of 'Have regard for . . .' or 'Take into account. . . .'. In real terms, the former phrase bears more weight than the latter. The principal legislation containing reference to archaeology is:

Coal Mining Subsidence Act 1957: Section 9(1) requires British Coal to restore to its former condition any Scheduled Ancient Monument damaged by subsidence resulting from underground coal mining.

Land Powers Defence Act 1958: Section 6(4b) is intended to ensure that no damage occurs to any Scheduled Ancient Monument when military training is carried out upon private land.

Mines (Working Facilities and Support) Act 1966: Section 7(8) provides for appropriate support for Scheduled Ancient Monuments via planning restrictions on mines or mineral working where their preservation is likely to be under threat from inadequate support as a result of mining or mineral working.

Forestry Act 1967: Section 40(2) prevents the Forestry Commission from compulsorily purchasing land which is the site of a Scheduled Ancient Monument or other object of archaeological interest.

Land Drainage Act 1976: Section 111 notes that nothing in the Act authorises anyone to do anything that is in contravention of the Ancient Monuments legislation.

Electricity Act 1989: Schedule 9 of the Act requires licence holders to 'have regard for the desirability of protecting sites, buildings (including structures) and objects of architectural, historic or archaeological interest'.

Water Industry Act 1991: In Part 1, Section 3.2 there is a requirement to have regard to the desirability of protecting and conserving buildings, sites and objects of archaeological, architectural or historic interest; and a requirement to take into account any effect which proposals would have on the beauty or amenity of any rural or urban area or on any such flora, fauna, features, buildings, sites or objects.

Recent legislation and planning policy

Town and Country Planning legislation continues to evolve. The *Planning and Compensation Act 1991* clarifies points in the *Town and Country Planning Act 1990*. It places an onus upon archaeological bodies and officers to ensure that due consideration is given to archaeology and historic buildings and structures within development plans. The 1991 Act also charges English Heritage and English Nature as statutory consultees in the development plan process.

The *Town and Country Planning (General Permitted Development) Order 1995*, an amendment to the *General Development Order 1988*, came into force on 3 June 1995. This Order (Statutory Instrument 1995/418) includes the following definition of a site of archaeological interest: 'Land which is included in the Schedule of Monuments compiled by the Secretary of State under Section 1 of the Ancient Monuments and Archaeological Areas Act 1979 (Schedule of Monuments) or is within an area of land which is designated as an Area of Archaeological Importance under Section 33 of that Act (designation of Areas of Archaeological Importance) or which is within a site registered in any record adopted by resolution by a county council and known as a County Sites and Monuments Record'. Under paragraph 7(2) a mineral planning authority may direct that planning permission is required for certain types of mineral exploration on land within a site of archaeological interest (see Griffiths, this volume, for a more detailed discussion of minerals extraction and archaeology). Paragraph 10 (Statutory Instrument 1995/419) requires a planning authority, before granting planning permission, to consult English Heritage on development likely to affect the site of a Scheduled Ancient Monument or a Grade I or Grade II* park or garden on the English Heritage Parks and Gardens Register. Part 26 of the Order covers permitted development status for development by or on behalf of English Heritage on buildings or monuments in its guardianship or owned, controlled or managed by it.

The *Environment Act 1995* has incorporated many called-for changes to environmental legislation. It has created the Environment Agency for England and Wales, a new body which assumes the responsibilities of the former National Rivers Authority and Her Majesty's Inspectorate of Pollution. The Act is also the enabling legislation to establish new autonomous National Parks Authorities (see Smith, this volume). Archaeology and historic features come under Section 7:

> 'to further the conservation and enhancement of natural beauty and the conservation of flora, fauna and geological or physiographic features of special interest and also to have regard to the desirability of protecting and conserving buildings, sites and objects of archaeological, architectural, engineering or historic interest'.

Section 97 provides for the Hedgerows Regulations and Section 98 for grants to manage hedgerows that are conducive to the conservation or enhancement of the natural beauty or amenity of the countryside (including its flora and fauna and geological and physiographic features) or of any features of archaeological interest.

The *Hedgerows Regulations* came into force on 1 June 1997 under Statutory Instrument No. 1160. The Regulations apply to any hedgerow growing in, or adjacent to, any common land, protected land or land used for agriculture, forestry or the breeding or keeping of horses, ponies or donkeys, if: (a) it has a continuous length of or exceeding 20 metres; or (b) it has a continuous length of less than 20 metres and, at each end, meets (whether by intersection or junction) another hedgerow.

A hedgerow is deemed historically 'important' if it (a) has existed for 30 years or more; and (b) satisfies at least one of the following criteria:

1. The hedgerow marks the boundary, or part of the boundary, of at least one historic parish or township; and for this purpose 'historic' means existing before 1850.

2. The hedgerow incorporates a Scheduled Ancient Monument or an archaeological feature recorded in a Sites and Monuments Record (SMR).

3. The hedgerow forms the boundary of a pre-1600 AD estate or manor recorded in an SMR or an archive held at a Record Office, or can be seen to be related to a building or other feature of a pre-1600 AD estate or manor.

4. Where there is documentary evidence for the hedgerow forming an integral part of a pre-Inclosure Acts field system, or can be seen to be related to a building or other feature related with such a system, which is virtually complete or is of a pattern deemed to be a key landscape characteristic by a Local Planning Authority.

Before a hedgerow can be destroyed a removal notice must be lodged with the Local Planning Authority in advance of the work. The Local Planning Authority has 42 days in which to decide whether the hedgerow is important. If this is the case, it will issue a hedgerow retention notice. The penalty for unauthorised removal of a hedgerow, irrespective of whether it is important or not, is an unlimited fine and an order to replace the hedgerow. Isolated fragments of hedgerow less than 20 metres long or hedgerows in private gardens are not covered by the Regulations.

Sustainability: a new philosophy for the 1990s?

In 1990 the Conservative Government issued its White Paper *This Common Inheritance: Britain's Environmental Strategy* (Department of the Environment 1990b) as a response to the Rio Summit (Quarrie 1992). The Government claimed that the White Paper introduced the philosophy of sustainability into policy-making: in particular that connected with planning. Two notable spin-offs for the conservation management of historic landscapes emerged from *This Common Inheritance*. The success of the ESA scheme, at that time three years into its pilot phase, prompted the Government to introduce another environmental management scheme which was not restricted to designated areas. While resisting pressure from environmental groups effectively to declare the whole country an ESA, the Government directed the Countryside Commission to introduce the Countryside Stewardship Scheme, which was initially restricted to a suite of defined landscape types, such as lowland heath and chalk grassland, where farmers would be paid to manage their land according to a predefined set of management prescriptions against a menu-type payment scale. The principal difference between the Countryside Stewardship

Scheme and ESAs was that within the designated ESAs all farmers were eligible to join, but farmers wishing to enter the Countryside Stewardship Scheme had no guarantee that their proposals would be accepted. Two years into the trial five-year scheme, a special category for Historic Landscapes was offered. In a similar manner to the ESA Scheme, there was the recognition at last that the historic environment needed positive management in the same way as wildlife habitats. Countryside Stewardship sought to combine as many different ecological/historical benefits as possible within each agreement, additionally seeking to offer new public access to hitherto private land. At the completion of the five-year trial period, the Countryside Stewardship Scheme was handed over to MAFF to be run in tandem with the ESA scheme. By March 1996 more than 90,000 hectares of land had been taken into the Scheme (see Figure 1.2 of this volume).

This Common Inheritance also offered an invitation to English Heritage to prepare a non-statutory list of historic landscapes in the hope that an inventory of the best and most representative might be compiled. A consultation paper appeared in 1991 (English Heritage 1991) with proposed criteria and selection methodologies. Although a list of historic landscapes along the lines of the English Heritage *Historic Parks and Gardens Register* was proposed, this approach was not considered appropriate and it was decided that individual LPAs should decide what was most important in their areas. A typical response is that developed by Surrey County Council in the ongoing identification and designation of Areas of Historic Landscape Value (AHLV). Here, potential areas which might qualify for AHLV status are examined against a set of selection criteria. Information is gathered to inform landowners and land managers of beneficial and harmful practices. The designation also acts as a means of gathering information which can be input into the county Structure Plan and also used in the consideration of planning proposals.

Current trends: the landscape character approach

There have been at least three attempts to classify the landscape this century. Dudley Stamp undertook the first modern land utilisation survey in the 1930s (Stamp 1946) and there was another attempt, albeit 'unofficial', by Alice Coleman in 1960 (Coleman and Maggs 1965). MAFF introduced the Agricultural Land Classification in 1966 to determine the quality of agricultural land and this system is still used by Local Planning Authorities. Classifying the landscape in order to inform planners of its amenity and ecological attributes has become a major thrust of recent Countryside Commission activity. In 1991 the Commission published *Assessment and Conservation of Landscape Character* (Countryside Commission 1991) which stated that the landscape character approach represented a valuable tool for, amongst other things, identifying valued landscapes for conservation and determining their management needs.

The integration of conservation and development issues in strategic plans is proposed by the Countryside Commission, English Heritage and English Nature in their joint publication *Conservation Issues in Strategic Plans* (Countryside Commission 1993). They call for the use of landscape assessment as the basis of decision-making in the countryside, utilising information from Sites and Monuments Records, archaeological constraint maps, landscape and habitat surveys.

In 1994 the first phase of *The New Map of England* appeared (Countryside Commission 1994). Building upon the pilot Warwickshire Landscapes Project, which established a suite of methodologies for analysing landscape components, the New Map project applied the landscape analysis approach to England as a whole, taking the southwestern peninsula for its initial focus. Concurrently English Nature was developing its own 'Natural Areas' approach to landscape assessment. The two projects were then combined, and with an input from English Heritage, the Countryside Character Programme was developed (see Cooke, this volume). Under the title *The Character of England: Landscape, Wildlife and Natural Features* (English Nature and the Countryside Commission 1996), the Character Map provides a bridge between national policies and the grass roots level. Evidence that the Countryside Commission was increasingly acknowledging the historic landscape in its thinking can be seen in the Working Paper *Views from the Past* (Countryside Commission 1996). In the paper, landscape assessment is proposed as the way of incorporating historic landscape character into Countryside Commission programmes and subsequently the framework for landscape planning and management.

PPG15 recommends the use of landscape assessment methodologies, in particular the Countryside Commission's Landscape Assessment Guidance and the Countryside Character Programme. Such approaches enable planners to identify where and how agri-environment schemes might best be extended and targeted to specific parts of the country and help in decision-making about the siting and composition of new woodland and, importantly, with the formulation of management strategies for historic landscapes. The Landscape Character approach acknowledges the importance of local distinctiveness and highlights opportunities to develop integrated strategies for the management of the cultural landscape. The Countryside Character Programme will provide a means of undertaking detailed historic assessment work at both national and regional levels as a means of providing vital information for the planning process.

The Rural White Paper *Rural England: a Nation Committed to a Living Countryside* which appeared in October 1995 (Department of the Environment/MAFF 1995) was disappointing in its apparent lack of awareness of the historic environment. Whilst considering the countryside to be an asset, no specific objectives were set out to address the needs of its historic components. The sequel to the 1995 White Paper, *Rural England 1996* (Department of the Environment/MAFF 1996) went a little further in that it mentioned the capacity of English Heritage's Monuments at Risk Survey for compiling the vital, high-quality factual information needed to guide strategic planning and development control. Yet still there was an absence of firm commitment towards the conservation of historic rural landscapes over and above that which has been described above.

Conclusion

Planning policies aimed at conserving historic rural landscapes are mainly incorporated within other objectives. The increasing awareness that the historic component of the landscape is more than the sum of its parts makes the outlook a little more optimistic than, say, five years ago. Agriculture is undergoing a phase of profound change with external influences such as the reform of the Common Agricultural Policy and increasing pressure to decouple support payments and replace them with environmental management incentives (see Potter, this volume). Many farmers are facing difficult times in the light of forecast reductions in farm incomes in the arable sector and the BSE crisis. It seems likely that the number of farms will fall and units will increase in size to gain economies of scale. Farmers in upland and marginal areas, where the preservation of historic features is generally better than in the more intensively cultivated regions, will become ever more reliant upon environmental management incentives in order to remain in business. In the likely absence of land-use planning controls the process of achieving positive and sympathetic management to targeted rural historic landscapes will rest with the Environmentally Sensitive Areas, Countryside Stewardship Scheme and their successor schemes. Landscape designation will continue to be a useful planning tool and refinements in management planning and implementation, supported by incentive payments, may provide a means of slowing the attrition of rural historic landscapes that has been a regrettable feature of the twentieth century.

■ ■ ■

References

Bromley, P. (1990) *Countryside Management*, London: E. & F.N. Spon.

Blunden, J.R. and Curry, N. (1988) *A Future for Our Countryside*, Oxford: Basil Blackwell.

Coleman, A. and Maggs, K.R.A. (1965) *The Land Use Survey Handbook* (4th edition), Second Land Use Survey, London: Isle of Thanet Geographical Association.

Council for British Archaeology (1993) *The Past in Tomorrow's Landscape*, York: Council for British Archaeology.

Countryside Commission (1991) *Assessment and Conservation of Landscape Character, the Warwickshire Landscapes Project Approach*, CCP 332, Cheltenham: Countryside Commission.

—— (1992) *AONB Management Plans: Advice on their Format and Content*, CCP 352, Cheltenham: Countryside Commission.

—— (1993) *Conservation Issues in Strategic Plans*, CCP 420, Cheltenham: Countryside Commission.

—— (1994) *The New Map of England: a Celebration of the South Western Landscape*, Cheltenham: Countryside Commission.

—— (1996) *Views from the Past*, CC Working Paper 4, Cheltenham: Countryside Commission.

Countryside Commission/English Nature (1997) *The Character of England: Landscape, Wildlife and Natural Features*, Cheltenham and Peterborough: Countryside Commission/English Nature.

Department of the Environment, Transport and the Regions (1990a) *Planning Policy Guidance Note 16: Archaeology and Planning*, London: The Stationery Office.

—— (1990b) *This Common Inheritance: Britain's Environmental Strategy*, Cm 1200, London: HMSO.

—— (1994) *Planning Policy Guidance Note 15: Planning and the Historic Environment*, London: The Stationery Office.

—— (1997) *Planning Policy Guidance Note 7: The Countryside – Environmental Quality and Economic and Social Development*, London: The Stationery Office.

Department of the Environment/Ministry of Agriculture, Fisheries and Food (1995) *Rural England: a nation committed to a living countryside*, Cm 3016, London: HMSO.

—— (1996) *Rural England 1996*, Cm 3444, London: The Stationery Office.

English Heritage (1991) *Register of Landscapes of Historic Importance: a Consultation Paper*, London: English Heritage.

English Nature and the Countryside Commission (1996) *The Character of England: Landscape Wildlife and Natural Features*, Peterborough: English Nature.

Keen, L. and Carreck, A. (eds) (1987) *Historic Landscape of the Weld Estate, Dorset*, East Lulworth: Lulworth Heritage Ltd.

Quarrie, J. (ed.) (1992) *Earth Summit '92: The United Nations Conference on Environment and Development Rio de Janeiro 1992*, London: The Regency Press.

Scott, Lord Justice (1942) *Report of the Committee on Land Utilisation in Rural Areas*, Cmd 6378, London: HMSO.

Smart, G. and Anderson, M. (1990) *Planning and Management of Areas of Outstanding Natural Beauty*, CCP 295, Cheltenham: Countryside Commission.

Stamp, L.D. (ed.) (1946) *The Land of Britain, the Report of the Land Utilisation Survey of Britain*, Part 62, Warwickshire, London: Stamp Geographical Publications.

Statham, D.C. (1982) *The Bransdale Moor Management Plan*, Helmsley: North York Moors National Park.

World Commission on Environment and Development (1987) *Our Common Future: the report of the World Commission Environment and Development (the Brundtland Report)*, Oxford: Oxford University Press.

Chapter 5

MAINTENANCE AND ENHANCEMENT: THE
MANAGEMENT OF ENVIRONMENTALLY
SENSITIVE AREAS

Peter McCrone

Introduction

Agriculture has been the major factor in shaping our landscape
during the past six millennia, overlaying natural topography with
archaeological and historical features such as field boundaries and
settlements and causing many of the vegetational changes which generate remarkable ecological diversity. On this agricultural overlay
are superimposed the remains of industry and past ritual practices
which, once abandoned, are affected by later farming practice.
The Ministry of Agriculture, Fisheries and Food (MAFF) is responsible for the implementation of a number of agri-environmental
schemes which aim to conserve the most environmentally sensitive parts of the farmed landscape (see Dormor, this volume).
The Agricultural Development and Advisory Service (ADAS), an
executive agency of MAFF, had responsibility for the technical
management of these schemes until 1 April 1997 when ADAS
was privatised and the Farming and Rural Conservation Agency
(FRCA) created to carry out the statutory duties previously
performed by ADAS.

Until the early part of the twentieth century most farming equipment and techniques would, generally, have been recognisable
to the prehistoric or medieval farmer with animal traction and a
large labour force working relatively small land holdings. The rate
of change to the countryside was generally slow (with a few notable
exceptions such as the laying out of extensive field systems as
on Dartmoor in the Later Bronze Age) (Fleming 1988) and the
removal of the traces of older settlements and land divisions, particularly in areas where stone had been used to build farms, field

boundaries and funerary monuments, was generally uneconomic in terms of the efforts involved for a limited return. The rate of change in the countryside began to accelerate in the eighteenth century with the development of early farm machinery to replace manual labour, changes in stock breeding and arable methods and in the eighteenth and nineteenth centuries episodes of enclosure in the champion regions which divided more open landscape of common fields and common land into smaller units.

The twentieth century has seen even more radical changes in farming. During two world wars thousands of hectares of land were ploughed to produce cereal crops in areas which had traditionally been managed as grassland, in some cases since prehistory: thousands of hectares of prehistoric field systems on the Wessex chalkland, for example, were obliterated. After food shortages during the world wars, the policy of successive governments was to ensure that Britain became self-sufficient in basic foodstuffs (see Potter, this volume). Particularly since the Second World War Government intervention has grant-aided agricultural improvement of land, particularly to 'break in' marginal land such as moor and heathland and to drain wetland areas. Technological advances in engineering led to the manufacture of increasingly powerful machinery to take the place of horse power and manual labour; the increased size and power of tractors and the use of bulldozers to level land meant the loss of individual monuments on a scale unseen in the days when horse power and manual labour were employed to clear land. At the same time amalgamation of fields by removal of hedgerows and walls, to allow more efficient use of machinery, eroded the historic fabric of the landscape. Liming, fertilising, ploughing and re-seeding of ancient grassland and moorland, with increased use of pesticide sprays, led to vastly improved yields but to the loss of many ecologically rich areas which had been the product of traditional grazing and haymaking methods.

The increasing concern over the environmental impact of agriculture (for archaeology epitomised by Darvill's *Archaeology in the Uplands: What Future for our Past?* [1986]) coupled with massive overproduction of foodstuffs which led to cereal, beef, butter and cheese 'mountains' in Europe led to the formulation of a European Community Regulation (EC/797/85) to try to arrest or reverse the damage being done to the environment and to help reduce production of surpluses. From this came Section 18 of the 1986 Agriculture Act which allowed payments to be made to farmers in return for environmental benefits. The designation of the first Environmentally Sensitive Areas (ESAs) followed in 1987. The ESA scheme designated areas within which farmers were eligible for grant aid to support environmentally friendly farming methods and its operation is the principal focus of this chapter.

ESAs are not the only weapon in the arsenal of the agri-environmental programme coordinated in England by MAFF. The Countryside Stewardship Scheme offers management agreements for specific landscapes, habitats and features in the wider countryside (MAFF 1996; see also Potter and Dormor, this volume). Other schemes include the Moorland Scheme (to encourage reduced stocking of moorland outside ESAs), the Habitat Scheme (to encourage habitat management and creation on former set-aside, water fringe areas and saltmarsh), Nitrate Sensitive Areas (aimed at reducing nitrate leaching in areas where groundwater sources are used for drinking water), the Organic Aid Scheme (to encourage conversion to organic production) and the Countryside Access Scheme (to encourage public access on set-aside land).

The ESA scheme

European Community member states were authorised to introduce Environmentally Sensitive Areas (ESAs) by the EC Council of Ministers in 1985, through Article 19 of Regulation (EC/797/85), subsequently modified by further regulations, notably EC Regulation 1760/87 and the EU Agri-environment Regulation 2078/92.

The ESA scheme was introduced in England by MAFF in 1987 when five areas were designated after the passage of enabling legislation (Section 18 of the Agriculture Act 1986) following the pilot Broads Grazing Marshes Conservation Scheme which was set up in 1985–6 after concerns over the threatened ploughing of the Halvergate Marshes in 1984 (MAFF 1989; Dormor, this volume; Potter, this volume). Further designations followed in 1988, 1993 and 1994 and there are currently 22 ESAs in England covering around 10 per cent of the agricultural area (Figure 5.1). Within these designated areas at the end of the financial year 1995/6, there were 7,479 agreements covering 409,962 hectares representing payments to land managers totalling £29,100,000 (Figure 1.1 and Harrison 1997).

ESAs are designated on the basis of the following criteria:

- the area must be of national environmental significance;
- its conservation must depend on adopting, maintaining or extending particular farming practices;
- farming practices in the area must have changed or be likely to do so in ways that pose a threat to the environment;
- each area must represent a discrete and coherent unit of environmental interest.

ESAs are administered by MAFF's regional organisation, with professional management by FRCA Project Officers who act as the main interface between farmers and the Ministry. The Project Officers are backed by teams of environmental specialists including ecologists, landscape architects and, in the south-west, an archaeologist. Each ESA is reviewed by MAFF on a five-year cycle; alterations to management prescriptions are informed by monitoring results, changes in broad policy (such as the introduction of the UK Biodiversity Action Plans [UK Biodiversity Steering Group 1995]) and the results of consultation with a range of non-governmental organisations. ESA reviews can also result in boundary changes.

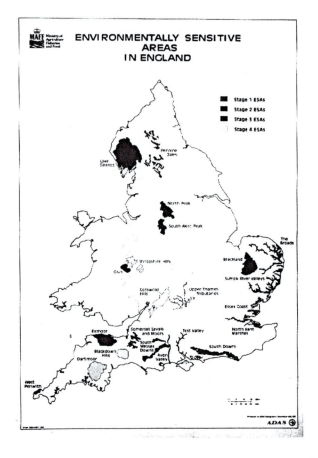

Figure 5.1   Environmentally Sensitive Areas in England. Courtesy of MAFF

A view of the West Penwith ESA (Figure 5.2) shows an extension made in 1997 to reflect the results of archaeological survey in the area.

Participation in the scheme is voluntary, with landowners entering into a ten-year agreement to carry out the prescriptions of the scheme (a set of management prescriptions for each area states the requirements for management of land under agreement). The prescriptions generally vary between ESAs and are formulated to protect the specific environmental interest of the area, although some are common to all. One of these ubiquitous prescriptions is that features of archaeological or historical interest will not be damaged, destroyed or removed, thus providing an element of protection to all the monuments on a farm, and often improving the management of sites where they can be taken out of cultivation. In most ESAs vernacular farm buildings (referred to in scheme literature as 'traditional') which are in a weatherproof condition at the time of agreement must be maintained. Each ESA has one or more tiers of entry, based on the environmental interest of the

Figure 5.2 A view of an extension made to the West Penwith ESA in 1997 to take account of archaeological features: 'clean' (i.e. improved) and 'rough' (heath) land, ancient field patterns enclosed by massive stone walls (Cornish hedges) and a 'round' or Iron Age/ Romano-British settlement. Photograph P. McCrone

area. Each tier requires different agricultural management regimes and these are set out in Guidelines for Farmers for each ESA. While a higher tier requires more from the farmer, with the aim of achieving greater environmental benefits, it also attracts a higher level of grant-aid, commensurate with hectarage and made annually.

In addition to these management payments, agreement holders can apply for Conservation Plans, which are two-year capital projects to enhance the environment. This can be work to improve the setting of an archaeological feature, for example:

● scrub and bracken clearance;
● reduction of animal erosion by fencing;
● structural repairs to derelict traditional farm buildings and field boundaries;
● hedge planting, laying, coppicing and banking to create stock-proof barriers;
● creation or reinstatement of ditches;
● construction of water penning structures (in wetland ESAs where tiers can include raised water levels for part or all of the year).

Although grants within a two-year plan-period are subject to formal limits, MAFF has the discretion to release monies budgeted for future plan-periods in order to allow major works, such as extensive repairs to buildings, to be completed. The percentage of the costs of the work grant-aided under conservation plans varies,

Figure 5.3 A traditional gate, manufactured locally, to a distinctive design (and with an interesting approach to filling a wide opening by an extension to the basic gate) hung on gateposts of local stone. ESA payments make up the difference between cheap, mass-produced, tube-steel gates hung on standard wooden posts and this locally distinctive vernacular gate. Photograph P. McCrone

with lower rates (typically 40–50 per cent) for items which are of direct benefit to the farmer, such as bracken control on enclosed land, but up to 80 per cent of costs for operations such as the restoration of traditional field boundaries, the protection of archaeological sites and works to allow public access. An Access Tier provides new opportunities for public use of agreement land for walking and other quiet recreation, paying for new permissive access to land and grant-aiding the provision of new stiles and gates (Figure 5.3).

For each ESA a broad strategy is needed to integrate all the environmental interests (archaeology, landscape and ecology) with the farming and land management needs of the ESA. This strategy is provided by a set of Environmental Guidelines which are drawn up to assist the Project Officers in the management of the scheme on the ground. The framework for the guidelines is a landscape assessment for the ESA which identifies and describes its overall landscape character and discriminates particular combinations of habitats and distinctive cultural patterns. This allows for the formulation of specific guidelines for management which will maintain the environmental value of each zone. Management decisions must take into account effects on all the environmental interests, removing the possibility that, for example, management of an archaeological feature will damage ecological or landscape interests. Such considerations may be paramount in many of the upland ESAs,

Figure 5.4 Dartmoor National Park. A superficially 'wilderness' landscape is in reality the outcome of thousands of years of human activity. Within a short walk from the viewpoint of this photograph lie the remains of a nineteenth-century mine with associated ore dressing floors, evidence for medieval tin streaming, medieval and post-medieval rabbit warrens, prehistoric settlements and a ritual complex of stone rows and cairns. Photograph P. McCrone

which are now perceived by the general public as untouched wilderness, but in fact contain derelict industrial sites, medieval settlement and prehistoric landscapes. For instance, most of the Dartmoor ESA lies within a National Park (see Smith, this volume) and supports heather moorland of international importance in a landscape that draws millions of visitors each year, yet the landscape is the result of thousands of years of human activity (Figure 5.4). Management guidelines for each ESA may need some updating within the five-year cycle of the scheme, to take account of changing circumstance and new research, survey and policy change.

Environmental monitoring

Section 18(8) of the Agriculture Act 1986 requires that '. . . the Minister shall arrange for the effect on the area as a whole of the performance of agreements to be kept under review and shall from time to time publish such information as he considers appropriate about these effects'. To this end environmental monitoring programmes have been established in individual ESAs which are targeted according to the environmental characteristics and objectives of each Area. The aims and methods of this form of appraisal are described in the *ADAS National Strategy for ESA Monitoring* (ADAS 1995). The programme examines the short and long-term effects of the ESA scheme on the environment by establishing a baseline record of conditions when the area was designated and comparing this with information from subsequent resurveys at intervals.

Each ESA has a number of environmental objectives and associated performance indicators (MAFF 1994). For the first ten years of the scheme's operation the common, overall environmental aim for all ESAs was to 'maintain and enhance the landscape, wildlife and historical value of each area by encouraging beneficial agricultural practices' (MAFF 1992, 3). This has been refined in the light of ten years of experience in the Stage 1 ESAs to take account of the individual character of each Area. For example, the revised aim for the West Penwith ESA is 'to protect and, where possible, enhance the special landscape character of the area and its wildlife and historic interests, by encouraging the maintenance and adoption of appropriate farming systems integrating the clean and rough land'. (MAFF 1997, 3), where 'clean' is the local term for improved land, and 'rough' for unimproved heathland. These specific objectives bring together the particular management options within the scheme and apply to the whole ESA. The performance indicators specify targets which should be achieved in the five-year period following the initial launch or relaunch after a quinquennial review.

Monitoring is carried out by examining a random sample of each ESA equivalent to three per cent of its total area. Sample areas are selected to be broadly representative of the ESA in terms of proportions of the different landscape types and generally include both land which is under agreement and land which is not (although some ESAs have such a high uptake that non-agreement land often does not fall within sample areas). Sampling strategies are tailored to address the ESA objectives and performance indicators and other factors can be taken into account when establishing the baseline surveys (for instance the Breckland ESA contains large areas of Ministry of Defence training area and commercial forestry land which were omitted from the land cover base surveys because they are not eligible for the ESA) (ADAS 1995).

The landscape, ecological interest and historical and archaeological features are all examined with additional attention, as required, for special features of particular ESAs such as Raised Water Level areas in the Somerset Levels and Moors ESA (Figure 5.5). The landscape assessment carried out at the start of each ESA scheme provides a broad overview of the character of the whole area, together with a description and map of the constituent landscape types. The key characteristics of each type are identified and described in terms of the landscape elements that are present (such as hedges, stone walls, ditches, dykes or rhynes, field gates, traditional (vernacular) farm buildings and pollard willow trees) and their spatial distribution. This initial assessment provides a benchmark for evaluating the impact of change, enabling judgements to be made about the scheme's subsequent performance in maintaining and enhancing landscape character.

Figure 5.5 Wetland grassland landscapes are maintained by measures to retain higher water levels than those required by modern farming and by restrictions on the timing of grass mowing to improve conditions for breeding birds and species-rich grassland. High water levels also help to maintain the fragile archaeology embedded in the peat below the Somerset Levels ESA. Conservation plan payments to reinstate the pollarding of neglected willow trees help to perpetuate an ancient practice and to conserve a 'natural' feature which is as much a human artefact as more conventional archaeological sites. Photograph P. McCrone

Ecological monitoring covers a wide range of habitats and species. Monitoring methods are often specific to only one or two ESAs (for example lowland heathland occurs in only two ESAs, farm woodland regeneration is a feature of three ESAs and water-level monitoring is carried out in one ESA). Again, baseline surveys undertaken at the outset are used for comparative purposes. Full details of the biological monitoring methods are contained in the *National Strategy for ESA Monitoring* (ADAS 1995, volume 3).

Historical monitoring examines the effects of the scheme on archaeological features in two ways. The first is through the determination of land-use change and an assessment of its potential effect on monuments (for instance the conversion of arable land to low input grassland is assumed to have a beneficial effect on monuments while conversion of grassland to arable will have a detrimental effect). The second is through field visits to monuments to assess their condition, survival and rate of decay and identify beneficial changes in management which could be promoted by ESA management. Monitoring of archaeological and historical features is based upon a broad interpretation of the historic landscape, which includes ancient woodlands. Each ESA has an inventory of historical features which is derived from the appropriate county Sites and Monuments Record. The inventory includes only those sites which can be affected by agricultural management, and thus excludes domestic buildings, churchyards, most entries within villages and monuments in the public highway such as milestones and bridges. Two ESAs have included survey work to enhance their inventories by identifying historic features unrecorded by the SMR, and one ESA has a sample of features selected by the County Archaeologists of the counties within which it lies which may not therefore be representative of the ESA as a whole.

The results of monitoring the first ten years of operation in the first stage ESAs (Somerset Levels and Moors, Pennine Dales, the Broads, eastern South Downs and West Penwith) have been generally encouraging (ADAS 1996a, b, c, d, e). They have indicated that on land which is under agreement the environmental interest of the areas has been maintained. Where comparisons can be made, most monitoring identifies some damaging activities within the ESAs on non-agreement land.

Problems, conflicts and solutions

Complacency is not a problem for the managers of ESA schemes: monitoring has identified scope for incorporating changes to the schemes to provide greater environmental benefits in most ESAs. Some of these will be addressed by changes to the schemes as they are relaunched on the five-year cycle. An example of this is the problem of scrub growth on small archaeological sites where clearance payments calculated on an area basis have been inadequate to cover the costs of removal. A minimum payment has therefore been introduced in some ESAs (ADAS 1997). Other identified problems will require assistance and input from other organisations. One of these is the inadequacy of databases for some ESAs. In one ESA, at the time of survey for the baseline inventory, the SMR contained eleven entries for the sample areas surveyed. A survey by RCHME identified a further 29 features. The archaeologist carrying out the monitoring survey identified 338 historical and archaeological features (ADAS 1996b). MAFF's remit does not extend to carrying out large-scale archaeological surveys so these shortcomings need to be addressed by the English Heritage and the RCHME, to add to the already overwhelming demands being made on their resources.

Some classes of archaeological feature are less likely to receive positive management under the scheme. Ruinous industrial structures, for example the remains of mining and ore processing plants, are unlikely to be repaired by the farmer as the work is likely to prove expensive (even with a potential 80 per cent grant) and of no benefit to the farm (Figure 5.6). Landowners such as the National Trust may be more likely to undertake such repairs but for many sites intervention and 100 per cent funding by English Heritage or National Parks may be necessary to prevent important monuments from deteriorating into unrecognisable heaps of rubble.

Figure 5.6 A ruined engine house in West Penwith, on 'rough' land. This type of monument is unlikely to receive positive conservation under the ESA scheme but it is protected against deliberate demolition. On publicly accessible land it may be necessary to grant-aid fencing around such sites to reduce the possibility of damage to the monument and the public. Photograph P. McCrone

The continued subsidisation of production (see Potter, this volume) causes anomalies and contradictions in the system. Conflicts between different grant regimes are arguably reducing uptake of schemes in some areas and the amount of land entered into higher tiers, leaving potential for continuing damage to sites under cultivation. For instance, in one ESA where an early Roman iron smelting site under arable cultivation would benefit from reversion to grass, Tier 1 payments are £75 per hectare while the farmer can obtain £269 per hectare in Arable Area payments (in addition to the value of the crop) (1996 figures). Similarly, support mechanisms for livestock in agriculturally marginal areas leads to overgrazing of some upland areas. While this can actually be of some benefit to archaeological survey by reducing the masking effects of vegetation, the detrimental effects include increased risk of damage to standing monuments, erosion from animals trampling across monuments and local erosion around stone monuments which can be used as rubbing posts, particularly by cattle (Griffiths 1994).

A further problem is that the provision of grant aid to repair walls and buildings can lead to the loss of historical and landscape features on non-agreement land when, for example, ruinous walls are removed and the stone sold to an agreement holder in receipt of a grant, to be used in the grant-aided repairs. This however is not a problem faced by ESA schemes alone: more than one National Park

Authority is aware of similar problems with their own grant schemes (Smith pers. comm.). Wider protection of historic landscape features would reduce this, but may be difficult to implement, and the solution may be to require that recipients of grants give details of the source of their material, or to re-open some of the hundreds of small quarries which supplied the stone for many of the walls when they were first built.

Conclusion

The general trend away from agricultural support mechanisms that enhance production and towards those that emphasise environmental benefits through the establishment of agri-environmental schemes such as ESAs may go some way to remedying this situation. Further changes are likely as the result of further rounds of Global Agreement on Tariffs and Trade (GATT) talks and changes in the EU's Common Agricultural Policy, particularly as the EU expands, but the process of dissolving the contradictions at present inherent in the grant-making system will be long term. The current ESA schemes provide a huge potential for beneficial management of the historical elements of the countryside, including those 'natural' features which are largely the result of human management over centuries or millennia such as the heather moorlands of Dartmoor, the calcareous grassland of the South Downs, the wet grasslands of the Norfolk Broads and Somerset Levels and the heaths of the Breckland or West Penwith. This potential is gradually being realised as an increasingly large proportion of the areas eligible for the scheme come under agreement. The monitoring programme provides a mechanism for identifying necessary changes to ensure that the maximum environmental benefit is gained for each ESA. Uptake of conservation plan payments for the restoration of traditional field boundaries and vernacular farm buildings and to control vege- tation growth on archaeological sites is restoring some of the frayed patches in the fabric of the landscape. The rate of destruction of some of the finest physical, ecological and archaeological landscapes in Britain is being slowed and, in some cases, halted.

■   ■   ■

References

Agricultural Development and Advisory Service (ADAS) (1995) *ADAS National Strategy for ESA Monitoring*, 4 volumes, Oxford: ADAS.
—— (1996a) *Environmental Monitoring in the Somerset Levels and Moors ESA 1987–1995*, London: MAFF Publications.
—— (1996b) *Environmental Monitoring in the Pennine Dales ESA 1987–1995*, London: MAFF Publications.

—— (1996c) *Environmental Monitoring in the Broads ESA 1987–1995*, London: MAFF Publications.

—— (1996d) *Environmental Monitoring in the South Downs ESA 1987–1995*, London: MAFF Publications.

—— (1996e) *Environmental Monitoring in the West Penwith ESA 1987–1995*, London: MAFF Publications

—— (1997) *Somerset Levels and Moors Agreement Holders Newsletter*, Taunton: ADAS.

Darvill, T. (1986) *Archaeology in the Uplands: What Future for the Past?*, London: Council for British Archaeology.

Fleming, A. (1988) *The Dartmoor Reaves: Investigating Prehistoric Land Divisions*, London: Batsford.

Griffiths, D. (1994) 'Dartmoor: Erosion Control on Open Moorland', in A.Q. Berry and I. Brown (eds) *Erosion on Archaeological Earthworks*, Mold: Clwyd Archaeology Service in association with Association of County Archaeology Officers.

Harrison, M.D.K. (1997) 'Country case studies: English ESAs', in OECD Proceedings *Environmental Benefits from Agriculture: Issues and Policies. The Helsinki Seminar*, Paris: Organisation for Economic Co-operation and Development.

MAFF (1989) *Environmentally Sensitive Areas. First Report*, London: HMSO.

—— (1992) *The Somerset Levels and Moors: Guidelines for Farmers*, London: MAFF.

—— (1994) *Environmental Objectives and Performance Indicators for ESAs in England*, London: MAFF.

—— (1995) *Somerset Levels and Moors Environmentally Sensitive Area: Landscape Assessment*, revised edition, Oxford: MAFF/ADAS.

—— (1996) *The Countryside Stewardship Scheme Application Pack*, London: MAFF.

—— (1997) *West Penwith ESA Guidelines for Farmers*, London: MAFF.

UK Biodiversity Steering Group (1995) *Biodiversity: the UK Steering Group Report*, London: HMSO.

PART THREE

Users and their Objectives

Chapter 6

MINERAL WORKING:
A WINDOW OF OPPORTUNITY

Mike Griffiths

Introduction and background

Humans have exploited minerals since the Palaeolithic period.
Evidence for large-scale industrial extraction in the Neolithic is
well known from sites such as the Langdale axe factories in Cumbria
and Grimes Graves flint mines in Norfolk, a strange lunar landscape of craters and spoil heaps. The Bronze Age copper mine at
Great Orme, Llandudno, Gwynedd, penetrated some 70 metres
below the ground as a complex of shafts and lateral galleries. In
operation between 1800 and 600 BC, it is one of the largest known
in Europe. In Roman and medieval times the variety of minerals
extracted increased and by the nineteenth century most modern
minerals were being mined or quarried, some on a larger scale
than today. The archaeology of mineral extraction forms an important area of study in its own right, but this chapter will be more
concerned with the effects of modern intensive minerals exploitation on archaeological deposits generally and the specific controls
and mitigation strategies that exist to minimise the damage.

By the early twentieth century, urban sprawl increased the pressure to regulate matters for the common good rather than individual
benefit. Provisions finally appeared in the *Town and Country Planning
Act 1947* which brought almost all development under control
through the mechanism of planning permission. Since then there has
been a regular outpouring of amendments, legislation, policy guidance and structures to devise and implement policy. As development
pressures have become more complex, so the means of controlling
and moderating their impact has become more sophisticated, though
by no means perfect, as this chapter will demonstrate.

The demand for minerals over the last two decades has been cyclical, reflecting more general economic trends. In England and Wales the boom of the 1980s produced a 50 per cent increase in orders for aggregates, about 300 million tons in 1989. The economic decline in the 1990s has seen the need for all minerals fall quite dramatically, but as the economy improves, it must be assumed that demand will increase, particularly for aggregates. All existing and new applications to win minerals are the subject of planning and related controls, but these differ from normal planning permission as minerals extraction is seen as an intrinsically atypical operation in several respects: first, it is not an activity which results in a new land use, but is a continuing end in itself, and often a very long-term one. Additionally, mining operations are basically harmful and may render land unfit for future use. Finally, it is impossible to exercise choice in the location of mines and quarries: minerals have to be extracted where they occur. On the other hand, minerals are essential to society and those needs must be satisfied. For these reasons, minerals planning is operated through a unique set of regulations. These address two major issues: first that mines and quarries may be in operation for very extended periods of time; and second that it is necessary to restore the land when extraction ceases. Local authorities therefore have additional powers, in respect of minerals, to review and modify permissions and to require reinstatement of the land. The archaeological implications of minerals extraction are considered in various current Acts and policy documents and these will now be examined.

Current legislation, planning guidance and plans

Town and Country Planning Act (1990)

The *Planning Act 1990*, the latest in a series of updates of the 1947 Act, defines the main provisions for dealing with matters of land-use control and consists largely of a series of general statements of principle. Detail is provided by a series of orders, regulations and policy guidance issued by the Department of the Environment, Transport and the Regions. One important provision of the 1990 Act deserves note: it requires local authorities periodically to review all mineral workings, including old sites with unworked extensions, which must be registered within a specified time period. All mineral working permissions are limited under the Act, normally to a period not exceeding sixty years.

Ancient Monuments and Archaeological Areas Act (1979) and Treasure Act (1996)

The *Ancient Monuments and Archaeological Areas Act* (1979) (AMAA) and the *Treasure Act* (1996) are the only primary archaeological legislative provisions currently in force. All guidance notes, structure plans and local plans reflect the importance of scheduling as a means of protecting sites of national importance. Almost without exception, they assume that the presence of a scheduled site will constitute grounds for the refusal of permission for minerals extraction. In some places, the wording of the plans implies that this consideration will outweigh all others (an example is the North Yorkshire Minerals Local Plan). In reality, a scheduled monument is likely to be no more than one among many considerations: economic and social arguments in favour of development may win the day. Nevertheless, minerals operators were sufficiently aware of the significance of archaeology in their industry to produce a Code of Practice for archaeological investigations as early as 1982 (Confederation of British Industry 1991, 2).

It is expected that the Local Planning Authority (LPA) will consult the relevant statutory bodies before determining any application affecting a scheduled monument or its setting, and take due regard of the observations made. Even if planning permission is granted, however, it is still necessary for Scheduled Monument Consent (SMC) to be sought and in determining that SMC, the relevant Secretary of State is under no obligation to take account of the planning decision made by the LPA.

Environmental assessment

The *Town and Country Planning (Assessment of Environmental Effects) Regulations* 1988 represented the first instance of European community law having a direct impact on town and country planning law in the United Kingdom. The regulations implement the provisions of EC Directive 337/85 on Environmental assessment and they require that the potential environmental impact of a proposed development is assessed before it is determined and that the information is provided in support of a planning application. Environmental impact is clearly signalled here as a material consideration in the determination of applications.

The types of development covered by the regulation are not all-embracing. There are two lists of projects. Assessment is mandatory in the case of 'Schedule 1 projects', which include nuclear power stations, crude-oil refineries, roads, railway lines and inland waterways. For 'Schedule 2 projects' (including all forms of mineral workings), an environmental assessment is required if the impact is likely to be significant in terms of nature, size or location. Most modern applications for mineral working are in rural areas, involving large-scale operations which generate considerable traffic and produce permanent landscape changes: environmental assessments are therefore normally required.

The content of the Environmental Statement (ES) is specified in the Regulation. It includes the requirement to provide a description of the likely significant effects, direct or indirect, on the environment of the development. As well as the natural and human environment, it refers to the cultural heritage. This is normally interpreted to include archaeological remains, historic landscapes and features of historic interest (Ralston and Thomas 1993). The statement must also include the proposed mitigation methods to avoid, reduce or remedy any significant adverse effects. The ES can be submitted in advance of, along with or after the planning

application. Whichever it is, the LPA must ensure its advertisement, public availability and circulation to a number of consultees, including the relevant Secretary
of State.

The ES must be taken into account by the LPA when determining a planning
application but it is not deemed to have any greater significance than any other
legitimate consideration. Its material consideration must be weighed in the balance.
Where a planning permission is granted, an LPA must confirm that it has considered the environmental information, but it is not required to provide a statement
on the weight given to it in its deliberations.

Planning Policy Guidance

Planning Policy Guidance notes (PPGs) have been regularly issued in England and
Wales since 1988. In Scotland, they are known as National Planning Policy
Guidelines (NPPGs). Their purpose is to provide both general and specific guidance on planning policies to LPAs, and they constitute a material consideration
when determining an application. PPG1 *General Policy and Principles* was last revised
in March 1997. It outlines the Conservative administration's view of the planning
rationale, namely that applications for development should be allowed, having regard
to the development plan and all material considerations, unless the proposed development would cause demonstrable harm to interests of acknowledged importance.
In 1990, the appearance of PPG16 *Archaeology and Planning* gave the first real
indication that archaeological sites and historic landscapes constituted an item
of acknowledged importance in planning terms. Despite subsequent criticism of
PPG16, it remains a vital, if flawed, instrument of archaeological policy throughout
the United Kingdom, either directly or by inference. Its sister document for
Scotland, NPPG5 *Archaeology and Planning*, was issued in 1994. Along with PPG15
Planning and the Historic Environment, which deals *inter alia* with historic landscapes,
these documents provide the basis for all current archaeological and historic landscape planning policies at national, regional and local levels.

The emphasis of PPG16 is on the finite and non-renewable nature of the archaeological resource. The note proclaims that it forms part of our national identity,
is valuable in terms of education, leisure and tourism and should not be needlessly
or thoughtlessly destroyed. It provides a basis for a planning procedure that requires
the value of an archaeological site to be assessed, evaluated and any damage miti-
gated, irrespective of the nature, size or impact of the proposed development. In
effect, it encourages LPAs to apply many of the provisions of the Environmental
Assessment regulation to any proposed development site, irrespective of scale or
character, that can be shown to possess, or to have the potential to possess, significant archaeological remains or deposits.

As with all aspects of planning law and regulation, minerals are identified as
a special case. PPG16 recognises at paragraph 11 that archaeological issues will
have particular significance especially in the extraction of sand and gravel. It also

emphasises that minerals are a special case in that they can only be worked where they are found, so that the flexibility of choice in location is more limited than for most other forms of development. It might have added that unlike most other forms of development, there is also often little opportunity to use design strategies to preserve sites where quarrying is the method of extraction.

The central policy of PPG16 is that the most significant archaeological sites should be preserved *in situ*. This can be achieved either by refusal of planning permission in the case of sites of national importance, by preservation *in situ* where development is approved or, as a last resort, by preservation by record (i.e. excavation). The responsibility for applying these policies lies with the LPAs. Where archaeological potential is identified, it is expected that a prospective developer will arrange for an assessment and evaluation of the site and submit the results obtained as supporting evidence to a planning application. While there is no legal obligation to follow this course of action, failure to supply adequate information to allow an LPA to make a reasonable judgement is a valid ground for refusing an application. There is no guidance regarding what constitutes an adequate assessment so this is left to the LPA to determine. Once archaeology is firmly established as a material consideration, the LPA must be satisfied, before granting planning permission, that proper provision exists to protect its planning interests. This means that where a site is to be preserved *in situ* or by record, adequate provision must be in place to preserve the site or mount an appropriate level of archaeological investigation, recording and reporting. It recommends that this should be achieved either by prior agreement or by the imposition of a suitable condition. Where conditions are used, they must meet the tests of reasonableness set down in DoE Circular 1/85. The model offered is that of a 'Grampian type' condition, in effect a negative condition requiring the developer to delay commencement of an approved development until some other works have been completed. Such a condition in an area of archaeological interest would require that no development take place until a written scheme of archaeological work has been submitted, approved by the LPA and implemented. This is the most common type of condition used in such instances.

PPG16 also recognises that there will be instances where, despite a full evaluation and implementation of an agreed scheme of works, the full significance of the archaeological remains will only become obvious during development. In such instance, the Secretary of State could choose to schedule a site if it were considered to be of national significance or the LPA could revoke or vary the planning permission. In both cases, compensation would be payable.

The impact of PPG16 may be seen in the revised *Archaeological Investigations Code of Practice for Mineral Operators*: 'archaeologists accept that minerals can only be worked where they are found while the mineral industry understands that *in situ* preservation of archaeological sites is usually preferable to excavation. So a balance should be struck in each case to reflect the archaeological importance of the site and the extent to which its preservation would sterilise important minerals. It is recognised that preservation is not always possible, but that some sites are of such importance as to outweigh the need for extraction. It is hoped that the revised Code will assist in resolving this conflict' (Confederation of British Industry 1991, 3).

Mineral Planning Guidance

Mineral Planning Guidance notes (MPGs) have been issued since 1988 by the Department of the Environment for England and they reflect the special place of mineral working in the control of land use. MPG1 *General Considerations and the Development Plan System*, issued in January 1988, covers the general principles and policies with regard to development plans. MPG4 *The Review of Mineral Working Sites* (September 1988) provides guidance on the review process and questions of compensation. Others deal with specific aspects such as coal mining (MPG3), aggregates provision (MPG6), reclamation of mineral workings (MPG7) and disused mine openings (MPG12). Yet others cover such matters as procedures for applications, compensation and control of noise. There is no MPG dealing specifically with archaeology, though several produced after 1990 refer directly to the policy advice in PPG16, and, since 1994 they have taken account of PPG15.

Structure plans

Structure plans are intended to provide broad land-use policies, but not detailed land allocation, for the area they cover. The policies cover development and use of land, including measures to improve the physical environment and management of traffic. They cover all forms of development including minerals. All structure plans include a section dealing with the winning and working of minerals, even when this is a minor feature in the economic life of the area. All structure plans include policy statements on archaeology: the following examples, taken from the Cleveland Structure Plan, are typical of the general nature of most structure plan policies currently adopted:

> Development which would adversely affect Scheduled Ancient Monuments should not be permitted and other sites of archaeological interest should be safeguarded from development wherever possible. Local authorities should encourage and assist in the investigation of sites of archaeological interest and should, wherever possible, safeguard them from development. They should be satisfied that sites of potential archaeological interest have been evaluated and, where development is permitted, the planning authority should seek to ensure that archaeological remains are preserved *in situ* or that investigations take place before development or demolition occurs.

> Local Authorities should seek to identify landscapes of particular archaeological and historic significance, and ensure the protection and enhancement of such areas by encouraging management schemes and providing appropriate information about such areas.

Minerals local plans

Whereas structure plan policies provide the broad statements of planning policy, local plans provide the means of fleshing out those statements and of identifying specific areas. All LPAs that are also mineral planning authorities (MPAs) are required to produce a minerals local plan. It must contain detailed policies for the area in respect of the winning and working of minerals and the deposit of mineral waste. The body that constitutes the MPA varies from locality to locality, depending on local authority structure. It may reside at county level, or within a unitary authority, or, in Scotland, at a regional level.

The minerals local plan should be in broad conformity with the structure plan but go into far more detail. The plans must also take account of national and regional policies as detailed in the various PPGs, of which there are currently twenty-four, the MPGs numbering fifteen and the thirteen Regional Planning Guidance notes. The minerals local plan must contain the evidence upon which the policies are based, relevant maps and any other descriptive matter as is deemed appropriate. Production of such a plan will normally identify areas of search for future mineral exploitation.

Set out below are the relevant policies from three northern counties and one of the unitary authorities. In each case, the aims are expressed as variations on the theme of protecting the historic environment. They all refer to PPG15 and PPG16 and reflect the main elements of each. Scheduled ancient monuments and heritage sites should be protected and recording must be agreed and implemented. While the specific wording may vary, the objectives remain the same.

North Yorkshire

Policy 4/3 Archaeological Assessment: 'The minerals planning authority will require applications for mineral operations affecting sites of known or potential archaeological importance to be accompanied by an archaeological field evaluation including a proposed mitigation strategy.'

Policy 4/8 Archaeological Sites: 'Proposals for mineral operations which would adversely affect nationally important archaeological remains, whether scheduled or not, and their settings, or other sites of special local or regional importance, will not be permitted.'

Policy 4/9 Other Heritage Features: 'Proposals for mineral operations will be permitted only where there would be no significant adverse effects on listed buildings, registered parks, gardens and historic battlefields or conservation areas including their settings.'

Northumberland

Policy EP6: 'The assessment of proposals for mineral working will take into account their impact on sites and buildings of historic importance. Proposals which would adversely affect nationally important historical sites or buildings and their settings will not be permitted other than in exceptional circumstances. Where proposals would affect regional or locally important historical sites or buildings, account will need to be taken of the need for the minerals, the availability of alternative sites or materials and the degree to which a mineral operation can be designed to minimise damage to such areas.'

Policy EP7: 'Where proposals for mineral workings affect sites of known or potential archaeological importance, or where the relative importance of such a site is unclear, the developer will be required to provide further information in the form of an archaeological assessment and where appropriate an evaluation. Where necessary an appropriate scheme of treatment will need to be agreed.'

County Durham

Policy M21: 'Where there is reason to believe that archaeological remains may exist within or in the vicinity of the site of a proposed mineral development, developers should provide an archaeological field assessment prior to the determination of the planning application.'

Policy M22: 'Where nationally or regionally important archaeological remains, whether scheduled or not, and their settings, are affected by a proposed mineral development there will be a presumption in favour of their preservation *in situ*.'

Policy M23: 'Where preservation of archaeological remains *in situ* is not appropriate, planning permission will not be granted unless satisfactory provision has been made for the excavation and recording of the remains. Such excavation and recording should be carried out before development commences.'

Gateshead Borough Plan

Policy E17: 'There will be a presumption against permission being granted for development where this would result in harm to a Scheduled Ancient Monument and/or its setting. Permission for development will only be granted where there is clear and convincing evidence that appropriate measures are included to preserve, and in appropriate circumstances enhance, the monument and its setting.'

Policy E18: 'Where sites and monuments of local importance are affected by proposed development, consideration will be given to whether they should be preserved. Where preservation of remains is not feasible, excavation for the purpose of recording will be sought.'

Case studies

All planning policy statements are, of necessity, general in their nature. They rarely deal with specific sites other than the most exceptional. Consequently, where a planning permission is sought to win a mineral, the specific circumstances relating to the site will have to be analysed in detail. In the case of known archaeological sites or areas of archaeological potential, this will normally require that considerable documentary and ground assessment be undertaken before the application is determined. Failure to provide enough evidence to determine an application can be a reason for refusal.

Where permission is granted, it is normal for any archaeological works to be provided for in the form of a condition or, less frequently, a Section 106 agreement. Under Section 106 of the *Town and Country Planning Act 1990*, a developer may enter into an obligation, by agreement, with either the LPA or the Secretary of State, to carry out certain works on, or even off, the site. The agreement must be covered by a deed, may itself be subject to conditions and the terms can be enforced by the LPA. Whereas most conditions require that archaeological works are completed before development commences this is usually impossible to apply on a mineral working, which will often be approved as a phased operation of winning and restoration. The 'scheme of archaeological work' tends, therefore, to be very comprehensive in nature and involve a phased implementation.

The following are case studies of three sites in North Yorkshire where planning permission is being sought, or has been granted, for mineral working. Two involve surface quarrying and another deep mining for coal. In each case the presence of known or potential important archaeological features has formed a significant factor in the process of seeking, gaining and implementing a planning permission.

An application has been submitted recently to win coal from a deep mine within the existing Selby complex. The area involved is being actively mined. The current permission was granted in the 1970s and the area has already suffered subsidence. When the first application was submitted the environmental requirements were virtually non-existent. Today the application has to face the far more rigorous requirements of an Environmental Impact Assessment and there is vocal opposition to it from the ecological lobby. A detailed study has shown that the area includes several square kilometres of major archaeological remains. The vast majority is represented as cropmarks but there is also an extant Bronze Age barrow cemetery, two Iron Age upstanding square barrow cemeteries, and a moated site, all of which are scheduled. There is also a church tower of late Saxon date and a number of listed buildings. The results of a preliminary study clearly identified the cultural heritage as a major constraint on proposals to extract further coal from the area. This has led to the preparation of a more detailed study with proposals in place to carry out large-scale ground evaluation.

Subsequent analysis of geological, engineering and hydrological data relating to the potential impact on the cultural heritage has shown that subsidence, which was initially assumed to be the most significant consideration, is unlikely to have any direct effect. The nature of modern deep-mining techniques means that the reduction in land levels is controlled rather than catastrophic and has, to date, produced no deleterious effects on structures such as the church tower or listed buildings.

The threat to the cultural heritage does not come from subsidence but from the mitigation measures needed to preserve the *status quo*, in particular current land-use and drainage regimes. Overall reduction in ground level within the area will be about two metres. This will lead to some drainage being impeded, causing localised problems. Over much of the area, it is possible that the archaeological sites will become wetter, theoretically increasing the potential for long-term preservation. Unfortunately, this would reduce the agricultural value of a number of important areas and cause severe disruption to internationally important bird and flora habitats, so the problem will have to be countered. It may be necessary, therefore, to improve existing field and land drains and in some instances pumping resources. The construction of these remedial works could have a severe impact on significant archaeological remains.

The planning application will be the subject of detailed analysis by the MPA. It will have to face balancing the demand for coal against the environmental impact. The current evidence suggests that mitigation strategies for archaeology and natural habitats are, in some places, mutually damaging and so the conflict is likely to be between the different cultural and ecological interests trying to maintain the *status quo*. What may prove necessary for the well-being of the one could threaten the integrity of the other.

The area around Catterick has been extensively quarried for many decades. An application was submitted in 1994 for a small area, less than four hectares, which was surrounded on three sides by existing quarry works. Part of the site contained a fragment of a scheduled monument, the bulk of which had been destroyed by quarrying in the 1960s. Aerial photography had identified the presence of an enclosed settlement and a sample excavation of this in the mid 1980s had suggested that the site was probably Romano-British.

Planning permission was sought and granted subject to the implementation of a detailed scheme of works including total excavation of the threatened area and provision to deal with a series of 'potentials', including the possibility of an Anglian settlement. SMC was also granted subject to the same conditions. Excavation proved the enclosure to be Iron Age in date, the Anglian site was found to be occupied by a massive bank of river cobbles, virtually invisible until sectioned. This was a portion of the bank of a Roman *ludus*, a military amphitheatre, the larger part of which lay outside the permitted area. Despite many years of archaeological research and fieldwork in the Catterick area, the site had not been recognised previously.

In view of the national importance of the site, an opportunity was offered to English Heritage to schedule it and remove it from the workings, subject to compensation being paid. This was declined and the quarry operator agreed to meet the additional archaeological costs that removal and recording of the *ludus* required. A further surprise was in store. On excavation, the bank of the *ludus* was found to incorporate the lower part of an early Bronze Age cairn, some 30 metres in diameter. This was also excavated and recorded. The site was treated exactly as PPG16 had intended, including provision to deal with unexpected discoveries. Consequently, the excavation has contributed a mass of new data that will require a major review of both the prehistoric and Roman occupation of the Catterick area.

Some miles further to the south, on the terrace of the River Ure above Boroughbridge, there is the largest concentration of major late Neolithic and early Bronze Age sites in Britain. There are five henges, at least one cursus, a major stone alignment, various pit alignments and a number of barrows. It is also one of the richest areas in the country for sand and gravel and has been exploited for several decades. This concentration of archaeological sites and its responsiveness to aerial photography has made it one of the most intensively studied in the north of England.

A proposal to extract sand and gravel from an area of nearly 80 hectares on the northern boundary of the main prehistoric landscape resulted in a demand by the MPA for an assessment of the potential archaeological and historical impact. A series of desk studies culminated in a field investigation. The results were inconclusive. A number of minor features, all undated, were identified. The MPA considered them inadequate grounds for the refusal of permission for what was otherwise an acceptable proposal. To ensure that any archaeological remains that might become known were dealt with, the MPA imposed a standard Grampian condition. As agreed, the scheme of work allowed for several different levels of archaeological response depending on the nature of any discoveries. The minimum requirement was that areas should be watched during topsoil stripping and that suitable records should be made if anything came to light.

Six hectares were stripped in 1995, revealing nearly 80 cut features of Neolithic date. They included pits and hearths. Many produced rich ceramic and lithic assemblages, though little environmental data. Subsequent watching briefs in 1996 confirmed that similar features occurred elsewhere on the site. In 1997 a conventional excavation in advance of topsoil stripping was carried out. This revealed an alignment of over thirty pits, which represented the major division in the landscape, possibly linking a settlement area and the ritual zone. Current discussions, as part of the general review of the quarry's workings are considering the need to alter the approach implicit in the original scheme of work, and to undertake more purely research-based investigations on selected areas in the future.

Despite the apparent paucity of archaeological remains revealed by the evaluation, the area's potential merited the imposition of an archaeological condition. The scheme of work required by the MPA covered the many different scenarios that might develop as the quarry workings were extended. Regular review has meant that it has been possible to develop the nature of the archaeological response. Currently the site represents the largest single block of Neolithic landscape examined in detail by archaeologists in the north of England. When finished, it will be one of the largest in Europe. It may well provide the answer to the vexed question of the function of henges, which may have been religious or trading focal points for scattered agricultural communities.

Conclusions

Mineral working has a dramatic, though sometimes transient, impact on the land-scape; in the process it can offend all the senses and sensibilities. By its nature it tends to be totally destructive, unlike many other forms of development, and it frequently coincides with areas of major archaeological and historical significance. Because of its impact, it is currently one of the most closely controlled and moni-tored of all industries, after nuclear power and chemicals. The publication of PPG16 in 1990 introduced a point of reference against which LPAs could develop their local policies. Before that, the use of planning powers to protect non-scheduled archaeological sites had been very patchy. While the historic city of Exeter had a policy in place as early as 1974, most LPAs were hesitant to interpret their plan-ning powers independently of central government until the publication of PPG16.

The current combination of legislation, directives, structure and local plans, minerals local plans, unitary plans and the raft of guidance notes should mean that no future mineral development escapes a thorough examination of its potential archaeological impact. Where permission to develop is granted, there is no excuse why an appropriate level of archaeological mitigation should not be in place before the first sod is turned. No doubt economic and other forces will sometimes outweigh arguments for the currently preferred option of preservation *in situ* rather than by record, but at least the conflicting views will be examined, normally in the public domain.

There has been recent comment from some archaeologists (for example, Biddle 1994) that PPG16, and its strict interpretation by some LPAs, is stifling archaeo-logical research. The argument goes that when sites are preserved *in situ*, rather than examined prior to destruction, the archaeological world is starved of new information. The criticism should be levelled against central government. It failed to inject the balance of the old rescue funds into research excavation as developer-funded archaeology grew. It is not surprising that developers choose, where possible, the cheaper option of preservation by design instead of costly archaeological exca-vation. Many mineral operators wish that they had this option but often it is not possible to preserve the archaeology without abandoning large areas of mineral, and so excavation becomes the preferred option.

The few case studies outlined above show that major archaeological discoveries are still being made in the countryside, if not in historic towns. A review of the major advances in archaeological knowledge over the last decade would, I suspect, be dominated by the results of work undertaken on mineral working sites. On many of these it is possible under the terms of current planning provisions to provide a structured framework for an archaeological investigation that can, over time, develop into a major piece of historic landscape research. In this sense, at least, rural archaeology is possibly making up for the bias of the 1960s, 1970s and 1980s when urban rescue work consumed the bulk of limited archaeological funds.

As a final thought, one must not forget that many old mineral workings, now mellowed by time, are seen as significant archaeological and landscape features, worthy of preservation. More obliquely, it is worth remembering that some quarries have become landfill sites and that future generations of archaeologists will have to seek their evidence among the stratified backfill of millions of black polythene bags.

■ ■ ■

References

Biddle, M. (1994) *What Future for British Archaeology?* Oxbow Lecture 1, Oxford: Oxbow.

Confederation of British Industry (1991) *Archaeological Code of Practice for Minerals Operators* (2nd edition), London: CBI.

Department of the Environment (1985) *Circular 1/85: The Use of Conditions in Planning Permissions*, London: The Stationery Office.

Department of the Environment, Transport and the Regions (1997) *Planning Policy Guidance Note 1: General Policy and Principles*, London: The Stationery Office.

Ralston, I. and Thomas, R. (1993) *Environmental Assessment and Archaeology*, IFA Occasional Paper 5, Birmingham: Institute of Field Archaeologists.

Scottish Office (1994) *National Planning Policy Guidelines 5: Archaeology and Planning*, Edinburgh: The Stationery Office.

Chapter 7

THE MANAGEMENT OF AN ARCHAEOLOGICAL LANDSCAPE ON THE ARMY'S TRAINING AREA ON SALISBURY PLAIN, WILTSHIRE

Ian Barnes

Introduction

Salisbury Plain Training Area (SPTA) is the Army's largest field-training centre in the United Kingdom. At 38,000 hectares, measuring 41km west to east and 16km north to south, it represents about 10 per cent of Wiltshire. It is the only training centre in the country large enough to allow unrestricted exercises using the Army's full range of vehicles. As well as being militarily significant, SPTA is also of prime archaeological and ecological interest. As will be described, the density and variety of archaeological remains on SPTA are outstanding in a lowland Britain context. It is the intention of this paper to show how as managers the Defence Estate Organisation (DEO), on behalf of the Ministry of Defence (MoD), strive to maintain a balance between military training and the preservation of the archaeological landscape.

Background

Topography and land use

SPTA is situated on Salisbury Plain, an extensive block of undulating chalk hills extending from Warminster in the west to Tidworth in the east. The training area is dissected by two rivers, the Avon and Bourne, both towards the east, whilst the western edge of Salisbury Plain is defined by the Wylye valley. The ground cover is grazed chalk grassland interspersed with areas of arable crops and forestry plantation.

The primary land use is military training followed by agriculture and forestry. Farmland is divided into two categories, Schedule I leased to tenants on a full agricultural basis and acting as a buffer between military training areas and civilian settlements, and Schedule III, the main training area, parcels of which are farmed to add an element of realism to the landscape for military training purposes. The forestry provides cover for soldiers and vehicles. Due to the inherent dangers of military training the public have only limited access to certain areas of SPTA. There are four sets of Byelaws on SPTA which detail the rules of access, copies of which are posted around the perimeter. Access to archaeological monuments can be arranged in advance.

Archaeology

There has been a wide interest in the archaeology of Salisbury Plain since the days of the antiquarian William Stukeley in the eighteenth century and Sir Richard Colt Hoare (Colt Hoare 1812) and William Cunnington in the early nineteenth century catalogued and investigated many of the major sites on Salisbury Plain including the most famous, Stonehenge, which is situated just to the south of SPTA. The majority of early work concentrated on the major ritual and funerary monuments, but there has been a gradual move to study the landscape as a whole. The aerial photographic work undertaken by Crawford (Crawford and Keiller 1928) before the Second World War and recently *The Stonehenge Environs Project* (Richards 1990), the Wessex Linear Ditches Project (Bradley *et al.* 1994) and a comprehensive survey of SPTA undertaken by the RCHME (McOmish and Field 1993, RCHME forthcoming) have highlighted the extent, and significance, of the surviving archaeological landscape.

In total 2,300 discrete archaeological sites have been recorded on SPTA, of which 551 are afforded protection as Scheduled Ancient Monuments. The extent and diversity of the remains on SPTA is remarkable as is their survival as earthworks which are acknowledged as some of the best preserved in western Europe (McOmish and Field 1993, 18). This survival can be put down to the fossilisation of the landscape since being taken into military ownership at the end of the nineteenth century with the resultant removal of extensive areas from the destructive effects of ploughing.

The earliest known archaeological sites on SPTA are Neolithic. A total of twenty-seven long barrows is recorded across SPTA, with a concentration towards the south particularly around the causewayed enclosure at Robin Hood's Ball. Over 500 Bronze Age round barrows are recorded over SPTA, many contained in cemeteries such as those known at Snail Down, Silk Hill and Milston Down. The extensive linear banks and ditches known over the whole of SPTA are also thought to be of Bronze Age origin. The Wessex Linear Ditches Project (Bradley *et al.* 1994) which concentrated its research on SPTA East concluded that these are likely to be territorial or ranch boundaries. It is during the Bronze Age that many of the field systems recorded across SPTA are thought to have been established. The Iron Age saw an intensification of activity with an expansion of the field systems over the majority of SPTA amongst which a number of settlements enclosures are recorded. During this period of intensive utilisation a series of hillforts was constructed along the edge of Salisbury Plain including the outstanding examples of Scratchbury and Battlesbury overlooking the Wylye valley.

The Romano-British period saw a continuation of intensive exploitation. Eleven major settlements are recorded, the largest on Charlton Down which covers 24 hectares; other substantial settlements are known at Chapperton Down, Knook, Chisenbury Warren and Church Pits. The settlements constitute the focal point of a concerted agricultural exploitation of Salisbury Plain, each being surrounded by extensive blocks of field systems. As yet there is no physical evidence of Saxon settlement on Salisbury Plain other than in the Avon valley. The later medieval period is characterised by lynchets on the scarp slopes; settlement appears to be confined to the valleys. It appears that the upland area was used for pasture during the medieval and post-medieval periods.

Ecology

The military occupation of SPTA over the past century has kept at bay intensive agriculture with its joint threat of ploughing and fertilising and has encouraged the survival of huge areas of unimproved grassland. This type of grassland was once widespread across the chalklands of southern England but is now found only rarely, SPTA being the single largest area in north-western Europe. The majority of SPTA is now designated within the following categories: Sites of Special Scientific Interest (SSSIs), a Special Protection Area (SPA) for birds and a candidate Special Area of Conservation (cSAC).

Military

SPTA is divided into three functional zones, SPTA West, Centre and East. The West and East are used for general exercises which deploy troops and vehicles, the Centre is dominated by the artillery impact areas which are fired into from elsewhere on SPTA. The East also contains areas where training is restricted when rifle ranges are in use. In addition to this general use of SPTA, certain discrete areas are allocated for specific tasks which include aircraft drop zones, landing strips, small arms ranges, demolition areas, urban fighting complexes, farmsteads, an engineering training zone and a cross-country driving area.

Management strategies

History of management of archaeological remains on SPTA

The first formal archaeological management on SPTA was as a result of a recommendation from a Defence Land Committee of 1971–3 (Ministry of Defence 1973) that a Conservation Officer and voluntary groups be set up to implement conservation work on MoD land nationwide. In 1979 the County Archaeologist for Wiltshire began to receive reports from the SPTA East Conservation Group that military training was causing damage to monuments in the area. These reports prompted a debate on the issue of archaeological conservation on SPTA generally, resulting in a survey to grade all the monuments according to their archaeological importance. The aim was to provide a baseline for management decisions on the protection of individual monuments.

The archaeological survey was undertaken by Wiltshire County Council's Archaeological Service (CAS) and the accompanying scoring of sites formed the basis of the Wilkinson Report (Wilkinson 1986), which was published in July 1986. This contained numerous recommendations which included the setting up of the SPTA Archaeological Committee, the production of management plans for a series of twelve areas of well-preserved and significant remains known as Archaeological Site Groups (ASGs) including seven Important and Fragile Sites (IFSs), and the issuing of basic guidelines for the protection of archaeological remains.

The SPTA Archaeological Committee ensured the production of the management plans (Defence Land Agent 1993) which were written in conjunction with the CAS. The Environmental Steering Group (ESG), on which English Heritage, the CAS, English Nature and other interested parties are represented, later replaced the SPTA Archaeological Committee as the policy defining body (Chadburn 1995). A subsidiary group, the Environmental Working Committee (EWC), was formed in 1994 to undertake the practical tasks involved in implementing the policies proposed by the ESG.

As part of the continuous review of conservation measures a Training Area Estates Management (TAEM) section, including an Archaeological Officer, was set up in 1995 to oversee all archaeological, ecological and planning issues on SPTA. In addition a Geographical Information System (GIS) was procured by the DEO to provide a tool for the monitoring and managing of SPTA, including the archaeological remains (Brown 1995; Coe 1997).

Threats

The main threats from military training are damage from the passage of tracked and wheeled vehicles, the digging-in of troops and vehicles and the impact of artillery shells. The potential threat depends on the vulnerability of the monuments and the intensity of training. The agricultural threat is the same as found anywhere else in the country: deep ploughing and erosion by stock. The threat from natural agencies is most commonly that of rabbits, which are rife on SPTA colonising many of the archaeological earthworks and causing rapid erosion. Trees are also a threat. In the past plantations designed for military training were established without regard to underlying sites. With the maturing of these plantations there is a risk of tree blow damage.

Levels of protection

Different levels of protection are afforded to archaeological remains depending on their importance. These are defined by criteria laid down by English Heritage and the findings of the Wilkinson Report (Wilkinson 1986).

> *Scheduled Ancient Monuments (SAM)*. These are defined as of national importance by the terms of the Ancient Monuments and Archaeological Areas Act 1979. The normal constraints for undertaking development work on SAM apply to users of SPTA.

> *Important and Fragile Sites (IFS)*. The military recognise that seven specific sites on SPTA are significant from a national perspective whilst being especially fragile and thus susceptible to damage. In these areas preservation takes precedence over training. Where practicable, as well as being protected as SAM, these areas are also placed out of bounds to vehicles.

> *Archaeological Site Groups (ASG)*. These are defined as groups or relationships of monuments and are designed to protect the wider historic landscape. In all, twelve have been defined over SPTA. Within these areas there can be no change of land use, particularly agricultural, without consultation. In addition each ASG has its own management plan in order to eliminate agricultural and forestry damage, to control damage by natural agencies, and to minimise damage from training. All IFSs are contained within an ASG.

For sites not Scheduled or included within an IFS or ASG it is practice to minimise disturbance by liaison between the military or agricultural user and the DEO. Where appropriate, monuments are afforded protection through local plans, and where development is concerned, they fall within the remit of the Department of Environment's *Planning Policy Guidance Note 16: Archaeology and Planning* (PPG16).

General management procedures

The management procedures concerning archaeological remains vary, depending on the perceived threat. The four main areas that concern archaeological management are:

- Military use,
- Agricultural use,
- Monitoring and restoration of physical state of monuments,
- Development/change of use.

The management procedures for agriculture, the monitoring of the physical state of monuments and development/change of use are basically the same as would be undertaken on a non-military training estate and as such are mostly outside the scope of this article. The management of SPTA is overseen by the multi-disciplinary

TAEM section in partnership with the military with whom they are co-located at the headquarters for SPTA, allowing a holistic approach to be taken. The TAEM section liaise directly with the statutory bodies over all proposals, thus ensuring a consistent approach. On agricultural tenancies management is undertaken through individual farm management plans, of which archaeology is one component. The physical state of monuments is monitored and managed by the various archaeological bodies with responsibility for SPTA, namely DEO, CAS, English Heritage and the Conservation Groups. Grazing, pest control and forestry proposals are all controlled so as to encourage the preservation of monuments.

Development and change of use is controlled by the same procedures as on civilian land with the additional constraint that all proposals are first vetted by the TAEM section. The TAEM section, as advisers to the military administrators of SPTA, conduct much of the preliminary work prior to planning submissions to ensure proposed developments have as little environmental disturbance as possible. As well as the normal PPG16, local plan and SAM criteria proposals are also vetted against any IFS or ASG status.

One of the main tools for the management of archaeological remains on SPTA is the GIS system. The DEO GIS holds all the data required to manage the estate of which archaeology is only one component. The archaeological data is based on the RCHME survey (RCHME forthcoming) and the CAS Sites and Monuments Record. All 2,300 sites are mapped at a base scale of 1:10,000, colour-coded by feature type such as bank or ditch and backed up with a full text entry. Using the GIS, the archaeological remains can be compared against other interests such as nature conservation, military training features or forestry proposals allowing rapid management decisions to be made.

Specific measures for management of military use

Although the prime use of SPTA is for military training, it is acknowledged that there are a number of nationally important sites whose significance dictates that their preservation takes precedence over training. In addition the military are committed to steps to guarantee that no nationally important sites will be deliberately damaged during training. The management of the archaeological remains is undertaken by the DEO in partnership with the military and, for training, can be divided into three categories: physical protection against damage, exercise planning and education. The management procedures for each of these are described below followed by a case study to illustrate them in action.

Physical protection against damage

With a total of 2,300 sites, large areas of remains on SPTA are vulnerable to being driven over by vehicles, dug into by troops or shelled. The basic tool for preventing damage from troops or vehicles is protection by physical barriers, whilst for shelling it is the management of targets. Within the impact areas there is the risk of damage from shell bursts. The degree of attrition has been reduced by the moving of targets away from monuments, particularly the extensive Romano-British settlement on Charlton Down in the Larkhill Impact Area.

The major factors in physically protecting monuments against troops and vehicles are scale, significance and training patterns. For example the physical protection of an individual scheduled barrow is a much simpler affair than protecting an unscheduled field system covering many hectares. In addition protective measures must not be a danger to troops or vehicles, especially those moving at night. All proposals for physical protection have to be agreed by the many interested parties on SPTA. The procedure is that proposals are put by the TAEM section before the Environmental Working Committee (EWC) which has representatives from the military, English Nature, SPTA Conservation Groups, English Heritage, CAS and land agents. At the EWC, any potential conflicts between the various interests are discussed and an acceptable proposal agreed. On acceptance the TAEM section ensure that all statutory criteria such as planning applications or Scheduled Monument Consent are satisfied and that the work is completed to an acceptable standard.

The use of the myriad earthen tracks across SPTA pose a threat to neighbouring archaeological remains. In dry weather tracks remain a single vehicle width, but in wet weather the situation deteriorates as vehicles attempt to avoid the quagmire into which calcareous soil quickly develops. New routes proliferate, and in a short time tracks can become up to 50m wide. Such proliferation is a threat to neighbouring monuments and two specific measures are being used to address the problem. Where the track spread is most serious, and sensitive monuments are located close to the track, the route may be hardened. Hardening a track involves the laying of a geotextile straight on to the present ground surface and the spreading across an 8-metre width of 600mm of stone scalpings. The building of such tracks requires the production of an Environmental Impact Assessment to support a planning application including, where necessary, archaeological evaluation of the routes. Drivers are then instructed to stay on the hardened tracks and thus the threat to neighbouring monuments is reduced. Where the potential for damage is less, perhaps because the track is less well used, but still present, then the less expensive measure of track restoration is employed. Restoration involves the maintenance of the track surface to stop the need for proliferation, and is undertaken by a combination of the filling of deep ruts with clean chalk and the disc harrowing of the route. Full consultation is undertaken with the TAEM section to avoid damaging any underlying monuments.

The hardening and maintenance of tracks is good procedure for protecting the wider archaeological landscape. It ensures that vehicles moving across SPTA do the minimum of damage both to the discrete smaller sites and the larger extensive sites such as field systems. However it addresses only one type of traffic on SPTA, when in reality there are two. The first is administrative and might consist of a set of vehicles moving to the start of an exercise, when the route taken is immaterial to the driver. This is not so with the second type of traffic, tactical traffic. Since the prime function of SPTA is to train soldiers so, when on exercise, military commanders in the field, at all levels, are left to make their own decisions. During an exercise, with the exception of the restrictions imposed by status as IFS, ASG or SAM for archaeological sites and certain other areas such as agricultural pennings, the troops have free range. In such circumstances, the emphasis for protection moves away from guiding traffic to physically enforcing the protected status of individual monuments.

The protection of individual monuments varies depending on the protective status, size and location of the monument. As a constant, all Scheduled Ancient Monuments are marked with 'No Digging' signs and, where appropriate, 'No Vehicle' signs. Yet signs on their own are insufficient to provide protection in vulnerable areas. Much training is undertaken at night, using vehicles with limited visibility when in 'fighting' deployment, so the chances of signs going unobserved are high. In order to rectify this a number of physical barrier techniques are employed.

The highest level of physical protection afforded is permanent penning. This involves the enclosing of vulnerable sites in permanent stockproof enclosures. These pennings are out of bounds to troops and the ground cover maintained by occasional grazing. Only the most significant sites, such as an IFS or a particularly vulnerable SAM, are afforded this protection.

A less intensive alternative to permanent penning is the timber palisade. This involves the enclosing of a site by means of timber posts spaced every 1.5 metres around the exterior of a monument, the top of the posts are painted white with 'No Digging' and 'No Vehicle' signs fixed at regular intervals. Wooden posts on their own will not stop a tank or armoured personnel carrier but the palisades are visible in the landscape allowing drivers to take evading action. The problems encountered at night are eased by the heat-retaining qualities of the timber posts which register as a different colour on the thermal imagery equipment used in nightscopes. Where there is a particular threat of vehicles hitting the palisades, substantial pyramid-shaped concrete blocks, known as 'Dragon's Teeth', are positioned in front of the posts in order to stop vehicles.

Palisading is an efficient way of protecting monuments. It does not impede the movement of soldiers on foot crossing SPTA and maintains the enclosed areas as part of the wider ecological landscape by allowing unimpeded access for grazing. The disadvantage is that only discrete sites can be protected. It would not be feasible to protect monuments such as field systems as large areas of SPTA would be denied to military training, but by virtue of their size these are less prone to serious damage since the dispersed nature of vehicle passages spreads the load and reduces the potential for damage to the monument as a whole.

A more indirect form of physical protection is the use of plantations to alter training patterns. Plantations are focal points for vehicles and troops on exercise: they provide cover for parked-up vehicles and are ideal for defensive positions. The management of plantation can, therefore, have a significant effect on archaeological sites. The removal of plantations may reduce the potential for damage whilst the sensitive positioning of new plantations can actively draw training away. In a similar manner the removal of scrub over vulnerable areas makes them unattractive to soldiers seeking cover and reduces the potential damage from digging-in.

Exercise planning

The broad objectives of an exercise are planned months ahead. This planning stage is an ideal opportunity to avoid damage to archaeological remains. Experience has shown that more damage is caused by tracked vehicles in wet conditions than at drier times, so it is now normal practice to book the larger exercises for the spring and summer months. In order to aid exercise planners, maps produced on the GIS showing Ordnance Survey bases, military training features and archaeological remains are supplied to allow sympathetic planning. In this manner the need to avoid monuments can be incorporated into the exercise; for instance larger sites can be enclosed in hypothetical minefields thus putting them out of bounds to vehicles.

In the field, commanders have a great deal of freedom. Troops and vehicles on exercise have unlimited access to the areas they have booked on SPTA. Digging-in, however, can be controlled. Troops dig in for many reasons but primarily for defensive cover, so these positions are predefined before the exercise commences. Close liaison between the military and the DEO enables careful positioning of trenches and thus damage to known archaeological remains is avoided.

Education

In order that damage to archaeological remains on SPTA is not caused by a lack of familiarity with their extent and nature or with the relevant protective measures, a programme of educating military users is undertaken. This includes the briefing of units garrisoned around SPTA and non-local troops on exercise. During briefing all soldiers are shown a film '*Plain Sense Too*' which details the importance of all aspects of SPTA, including the archaeology, and outlines protective measures and procedures. Each soldier leaves the briefing with a short *aide-memoire* outlining the 'do's and don'ts' on SPTA.

Case study: Chapperton Down

Chapperton Down is situated on a north–south ridge towards the east of SPTA West, overlooking the Berril valley to the west and Copehill Down to the south. The earliest monument on Chapperton Down is a Neolithic long barrow, known as Kill Barrow, whilst two Bronze Age round barrows are also recorded. Evidence of the extensive series of linear boundaries found over Salisbury Plain, thought to date to the Bronze Age are found across the area, the most substantial running east–west from the vicinity of Kill Barrow. By the late prehistoric period the landscape was also covered with the distinctive field systems which continued in use into the Romano-British period. Chapperton Down is best known for the extensive Romano-British settlement which covers some 30 hectares, and constitutes a series of house platforms aligned along a central street over a kilometre in length running along the spine of the ridge. At the end of the Roman period the site was abandoned and reverted to grassland which, apart from the occasional interlude of cereal farming, it has remained ever since.

The significance of the monuments on Chapperton Down is acknowledged by the layers of protection afforded to it. The Romano-British settlement is categorised as an IFS, whilst much of the surrounding landscape, including the funerary monuments, boundaries and field systems are incorporated into an ASG. From a national perspective the settlement and surrounding archaeological landscape have been designated a Scheduled Ancient Monument.

In recent years the monuments have been damaged. There has been serious rabbit infestation of many of the monuments, whilst the boundary ditches have been eroded where vehicles cross regularly. The settlement has been vulnerable to vehicles transiting out of the Berril valley and others seeking cover in the central holloway. This is because from a military training perspective Chapperton Down is located at a crossroads. At this point SPTA measures only six kilometres north–south, the IFS extending along one kilometre of this. The Berril valley to the west is much used for bridge engineering exercises; Copehill Down to the south is the location of the urban-fighting training facility; and the official crossing points over the Salisbury–Devizes public road are located close to the east. In addition the ridge on which the settlement is located is vital ground for armoured vehicles moving tactically and dominates a large area of the Plain. Given all the neighbouring activity there is great deal of scope for vehicle movement in the area.

As there were a number of conflicts of interest the solutions to the management problems were not straightforward. A number of proposals were put forward in the ASG Management Plan (Defence Land Agent 1993), whilst others have since been submitted to the EWC. To date the following have been completed:

- To warn troops training on SPTA of the significance of the area, and thus of their responsibilities, the IFS has been marked on the training map issued to all users.
- The north–south track to the east of the settlement has been hardened in order to move administrative traffic away from the earthworks. The previous north–south route which ran along the centre of the settlement was blocked at either end with plantations in order to divert traffic on to the new route.
- Two routes from the Berril valley to the west have been improved. An east–west route to the north of the settlement has been hardened to establish a route from the Berril valley bridge training sites. To the south another

east–west route over the settlement has been hardened to give an alternative route for traffic moving tactically.

- The IFS has been palisaded, with posts at wide intervals, to manage vehicle flows around the monument.
- Kill Barrow has been palisaded to stop damage from passing vehicles.
- A programme of rabbit clearance has been instigated to stem the damage from burrowing on several of the monuments.
- Plantations have been established around the major linear earthwork to the east of Chapperton Down in an attempt to encourage traffic on to established crossing points, which it is planned will soon be hardened.

To date the measures undertaken can be said to have been successful as the incidence of damage to the monuments has been reduced. Nevertheless, the area is constantly monitored, since ever-changing training patterns demand that management measures remain dynamic.

Future management initiatives

The management of the archaeological remains on SPTA is a dynamic process. The needs of military training are constantly changing as, for instance, in the development of new weapon systems which have introduced new vehicle movement patterns, whilst the withdrawal of troops from Germany has intensified training on SPTA. Both these developments have had significant effects on archaeological management.

In order to cope with all eventualities the management system needs to be flexible. The Wilkinson Report (Wilkinson 1986) and ASG Management Plans (Defence Land Agent 1993) addressed issues of their time. The latest management initiative is the development of an Integrated Land Management Plan (ILMP) for SPTA. This document will consist of a series of component plans for different concerns on SPTA, whose differing priorities will be addressed in an overall procedural section. It is intended that the ILMP will not be a document whose proposals are fixed to the time of launch, but rather that it will be a dynamic framework which will be continually updated as training patterns and conservation needs evolve. The ILMP is timetabled to be in place by the end of 1998.

To complement the development of the archaeological component of ILMP, several projects, conceived before the concept of an ILMP, were continued to fruition. The mapping of all archaeological remains on SPTA on the GIS was completed to define the baseline information. Allied to the GIS plotting, an assessment of the sensitivity of remains to military training is being undertaken by the CAS. For instance a ploughed-out monument is far less vulnerable to damage from tracked vehicles than one that survives as low earthworks. To this end the CAS are undertaking a complete survey of SPTA to assess vulnerability, with the information being captured on the GIS. When complete this information will allow sympathetic training allocation decisions to be made.

In order to justify the management measures recommended in the ILMP a series of studies is being undertaken to model the actual effect of training and development on the archaeological remains on SPTA. These studies include researching the effect of tracked vehicles on calcareous soils and the quantification of ground pressures under hardened tracks to enable a totally non-destructive track design to be formulated.

Conclusion

The archaeological remains and the threats posed to their survival are unique in southern Britain. It has taken many years first to realise the threat and second to raise awareness and to pioneer protective management techniques applicable to a military training environment. The archaeological remains are now managed by a partnership of the DEO and the military, in co-operation with English Heritage and the CAS, backed up by agreed management priorities. All parties are dedicated to preserving the remains whilst allowing training to continue as unhindered as possible.

■ ■ ■

References

Bradley, R., Entwistle, R. and Raymond, F. (1994) *Prehistoric Land Divisions on Salisbury Plain: The Work of the Wessex Linear Ditches Project,* English Heritage Archaeological Report No. 2, London: English Heritage.

Brown, G. (1995) 'Salisbury Plain Training Area (The management of an ancient landscape)', *Landscape History,* 17, 65–76.

Chadburn, A. (1995) '*A Procedural Framework for Managing Archaeological Sites on the Salisbury Plain Training Area*', unpublished report to the Environmental Steering Group.

Coe, D. (1997) 'Salisbury Plain Training Area: archaeological conservation in a changing military and political environment', *Landscape Research,* 22(2), 157–74.

Colt Hoare, R. (1812) *The Ancient History of South Wiltshire,* 1975 reprint, Wakefield: EP Publishing for Wiltshire County Library.

Crawford, O.G.S. and Keiller, A. (1928) *Wessex from the Air,* Oxford: Clarendon Press. Defence Land Agent (1993) '*The Archaeology of Salisbury Plain Training Area: Management Plans for Archaeological Site Groups*', unpublished internal report.

Department of the Environment, Transport and the Regions (1990) *Planning Policy Guidance Note 16: Archaeology and Planning,* London: The Stationery Office.

McOmish, D. and Field, D. (1993) 'Ancient Agricultural Communities on the Salisbury Plain Training Area', *Sanctuary,* 22: 17–19.

Ministry of Defence (1973) *Report of the Defence Lands Committee 1971–73,* London: HMSO.

Richards, J.C. (1990) *The Stonehenge Environs Project*, HBMCE Archaeological Reports No. 16, London: English Heritage.

Royal Commission on the Historical Monuments of England (RCHME) (forthcoming) *The Field Archaeology of the Salisbury Plain Training Area*.

Scottish Office Environment Department (1994) *Our Forests – the Way Ahead: Enterprise, Environment and Access*, Conclusions from the Forestry Review, Edinburg: HMSO.

Wilkinson, J. (ed.) (1986) *Salisbury Plain Training Area Archaeological Working Party: Report 1984–1985*, Bristol: Property Services Agency, Western Regional Office.

Chapter 8

WOODS AND FORESTS IN THE RURAL LANDSCAPE: CULTURAL HERITAGE, CONSERVATION AND MANAGEMENT

Tim Yarnell

Introduction

Woods and forests are a familiar element in many parts of the British landscape. They provide wide-ranging benefits such as timber, wood products, opportunities for recreation and employment, nature conservation, landscape enhancement and places for quiet relaxation. These have of course been provided at varying levels by woodland over thousands of years even though the scale of woodland cover has been drastically reduced.

Today there is an increasing demand for all that woods and forests have to offer. Generally referred to as 'multi-purpose forestry', the provision of the many benefits is encouraged in the management of existing woods and the expansion of woodland cover. Multi-purpose forestry forms a key part of local, national and international initiatives relating to sustainable development. Experience has shown that the pursuit of some benefits can have an adverse effect on other objectives. The purpose of this chapter is to map out the policy background and identify some of the challenges and tensions that have arisen. Particular attention is paid to the relationship between present-day forestry practice and the conservation of the cultural heritage, historic environment and landscape.

Significant factors to consider are:

- the impacts of past human activity in creating the landscape we see today;
- the diversity of woodland types;
- the objectives and aspirations of industry, individuals, groups and communities which have a part to play in determining the role of woods and forests in the landscape of the future.

Policy background

Forestry policy in Great Britain today should be seen in a global setting within the context of international agreements. Of particular significance are the Statement of Forest Principles adopted in 1992 at the United Nations Conference on Environment and Development generally referred to as the Rio Summit (Quarrie 1992; United Nations Conference on Environment and Development 1993). The following year in Helsinki, the ministerial conference on the Protection of European Forests developed 'General Guidelines for the Sustainable Management of Forests in Europe'. The Rio Principles and Helsinki Guidelines are wide ranging reflecting the diversity of issues relevant to forestry. Of particular relevance to themes of this publication are Rio Principle 8f: 'National policies should include . . . protection of . . . cultural, spiritual and historical other unique and valued forests of national importance' and Helsinki Guideline 6: 'Forest management practices should have due regard to the protection of . . . areas with cultural heritage'.

The United Kingdom Government set out the policies and actions that are being pursued here aiming for the sustainable management of existing woodlands and forests and expanding woodland and forest cover in *Sustainable Forestry: the UK Programme* (Department of the Environment 1994). Amongst the many objectives and initiatives outlined is a commitment to ensuring that important archaeological sites and historical features are not damaged as new woodlands and forests are created. How this can be achieved, given the history of the British landscape, presents particular challenges which are discussed below.

The history of woodland

Awareness of the extent that past human social and economic activity has influenced the present-day rural landscape has steadily increased over recent years. The significance of this human factor relative to wider conservation concerns and the need for a holistic or integrated approach has been the subject of several conferences and publications over recent years (Macinnes and Wickham-Jones 1992; Swain 1993; Berry and Brown 1995). These events have increased understanding of the context, location, nature and extent of contemporary woodland cover and some of the issues that may affect its future. This has been a welcome development for those concerned with forestry and woodland management.

The general history of woodland cover in Britain is one of extensive loss due to a number of factors from perhaps as much as 90 per cent cover around 5000 BC down to 5 per cent at the beginning of the twentieth century. No doubt there were episodes of expansion and contraction. A great deal of archaeological and palynological evidence indicates that much of the deforestation occurred in the prehistoric period. Despite this evidence and its presentation to wide audiences (Rackham 1990, 1994) there is still a widespread popular belief that extensive loss of woodlands is a relatively recent event. This belief has the loss starting with the Romans, intensifying as the refuges of outlaws such as Robin Hood were reduced and finally eroded as Nelson's navy was constructed. Similar perceptions have been examined in the context of Scotland (Smout 1997, 5–24). Here beliefs about the Great Wood of Caledon have led to a lively discussion between parties involved with the expansion of native woodland and its possible impact on the historic and cultural Highland landscape (Yarnell 1993; Breeze 1997). I refer to this particular example to illustrate that popular perceptions and beliefs about woodland can play a significant part in its future. There are many associations between people, woods and the past which continue to exert influence. Some of these issues have been explored in significant publications by Harrison (1992) and Sharma (1995). The titles of these works *Forests, the Shadow of Civilisation* and *Landscape and Memory* respectively, give an indication of some of the diverse factors that can govern responses to the wider rural landscape and are not limited to woodland.

Before looking to the future and woodland expansion I want to examine some of the issues affecting the management of the woods and forests seen in the rural landscape today.

Present woodland

Today woodland cover in Great Britain is around 11 per cent with the country cover of England 8 per cent, Wales 12 per cent and Scotland 15 per cent (Forestry Industry Committee of Great Britain 1996). This is a far cry from the 5 per cent at the beginning of the century and is largely due to the establishment of major forests in response to successive government policies of encouraging the establishment of a supply for domestic timber production. The problems that this expansion brought for archaeology and to the historic environment are well documented (Proudfoot 1989; Barclay 1992; Shepherd 1992). I do not propose to look back at this period but reiterate that many activities such as root growth, ploughing and scarification, road construction, use of heavy machinery and windblow can harm archaeological deposits. It is also worth remembering that some or all of these activities occur in all types of woodland, broadleaf or conifer, native and non-native, planted or ancient.

The archaeology found in existing woodland is broadly categorised as 'archaeology in woods' and 'archaeology of woods'. Archaeology 'in woods' represents the evidence of early land use and activities such as settlements, burial mounds and field systems before the present woodland cover became established. The archaeology 'of woods' represents evidence of activities associated with earlier woodland management including woodbanks, pollards, charcoal platforms and saw pits (Darvill 1987, 92–104). Once identified the conservation of archaeological features is dependent upon careful planning and management of the many activities which may occur in the wood or forest (Forestry Commission 1995).

Some problems which have to be solved may be more complicated than others. First, there is the problem of identifying the relevant features. Many are properly mapped and recorded in relevant archaeological records and if the manager is fortunate the feature is clearly recognisable on the ground in an area which has no trees on it. However this is not always the case and many features, although recorded as known to have existed prior to the planting or expansion of woodland, are often difficult to locate since they have been obscured by tree cover or with blocked access. A complicating factor is that some early Ordnance Survey archaeological records often recorded sites as being 'destroyed by afforestation' when in fact they were impossible to locate in unthinned young crops.

Archaeological sites that have been planted have usually been disturbed and damaged depending upon the method of ground preparation used and subsequent rooting activity but they are not necessarily without archaeological value. This is particularly true in areas of intense arable activity where survival of archaeology as earthworks is often only encountered in woodland. Another difficulty facing land managers which is not limited exclusively to those involved with forestry is the range of features, notably industrial monuments and later rural settlements, which are not yet routinely incorporated into archaeological records such as county Sites and Monuments Records, yet which should be taken into account when developing management regimes.

Development of systematic and practical survey programmes for tree-covered areas is one of the major challenges for the next few years. This is increasingly important as large areas planted in the 1950s and 1960s come towards harvesting. Technological advances, particularly the use of Geographic Information Systems, are proving especially useful but greater success will require the involvement of skilled fieldworkers and the communication of results to woodland managers. Skill shortage is a phrase often associated with problems in industry. We have to hope that it does not affect archaeology just at a time when efforts are being made to incorporate many aspects of archaeology into land-use management.

Major land managers such as the Forestry Commission, National Trust, the larger estates and, increasingly, the Woodland Trust have an important role to play in conserving important archaeological features and have adopted various strategies for achieving this. The Forestry Commission, the Government Department for forestry, has as its mission statement: 'protecting and expanding Britain's forests and woodlands and increasing their value to society and the environment'. The following section details how heritage conservation is incorporated into its work.

The area of forest land, which includes open ground, owned by the nation is managed by Forest Enterprise (FE), an agency of the Forestry Commission. Currently this land covers a little over one million hectares. Government objectives and policy are translated into corporate aims, objectives and performance measures and then applied practically in a wide range of situations taking account of the distinctive character of many forest locations. The issue of distinctiveness is an important factor when considering most aspects of rural, or indeed urban, environments and woodland of all types, shapes and sizes can contribute to this. The Forest of Dean is different from the New Forest; they both differ from Thetford which in turn is different from Kielder, and all contrast with Glen Affric. Differences are to be found in the history and traditions of the land they occupy, the communities that live there or nearby today and the uses made of these forests by visitors and indeed foresters.

Management of the cultural heritage within the Forestry Commission estate is incorporated into the Forest District Conservation Plan. In this, important archaeological sites are identified and appropriate management prescriptions selected to ensure their long-term conservation. In many instances this is a fairly simple process of marking out sites and controlling operations. Long-term management will certainly involve the control of natural regeneration or colonisation of the site by damaging vegetation and may include interpretation, presentation and public access. Doing nothing is not an option. Some Forest Districts have a considerable archaeological interest: the North York Moors National Park Authority, for instance, has developed specific projects to assist in implementing their Conservation Plan (Lee 1995). Similar projects are underway in the Forest of Dean, the New Forest and parts of Wales.

In order to measure its performance in managing archaeology, Forest Enterprise has set itself the target of agreeing with the national statutory archaeological agencies management plans for the Scheduled Ancient Monuments for which it is responsible. These numbered around 1,000 at the start of the process. It is intended to complete this process by the early years of the twenty-first century. In addition Forest Enterprise has undertaken a desk-based condition survey of the same monuments to be repeated from 2002. This will identify any improvement in the overall condition of the heritage assets and at the same time establish what the main problems to be tackled are and where resources should be targeted. At this point it may be necessary to reinforce the point that the Forestry Commission is committed to the conservation of all important archaeological remains whether scheduled or not.

Of course not all conservation measures will be as straightforward as those identified above. They have to be integrated with other multiple-purpose objectives including nature conservation, recreation and wood production. Occasionally conflicts arise: for instance how might a Bronze Age field system, unenclosed settlement and Iron Age hillfort which are now covered in a small-leaf lime woodland be managed? Although solutions are found on a site-by-site basis it is important that all the implications of management decisions can be assessed on a Forest District, Regional or National scale. For this reason the Forestry Commission has developed Forest Design plans which incorporate the information from the Conservation Plan, production forecast, landscape requirements, existing species composition and recreational use into one database. This provides a basis for enabling future revenue flows, harvesting and planting programmes and the range of potential environmental impacts to be obtained from the wider estate. Importantly this allows various options to be tested for their future impact upon wood production and environmental quality.

The procedures outlined above can be implemented on a large scale providing the corporate will and organisational objectives exist, but what of the thousands of woodland owners whose woods may be just a few hectares in size? Much of the history of woodland management and many archaeological sites are to be found in smaller mixed woods which are the responsibility of individual owners with diverse interests. Although many owners and managers are keen to support multi-purpose forest objectives, it may not be feasible to accommodate all of them within the resources available to the individual owner. The provision of adequate support to the owner of smaller woods is a significant challenge for the future. Support does not necessarily mean direct financial aid identified as compensation but can also include information, survey and advice.

No discussion of the existing woods and forests of Great Britain can ignore the issue of wood and timber production and consumption. The homes we live in, desks we work at and the not-quite paperless office are all part of the equation. Supply and demand will influence what trees are grown, where and why, well into the next century. The Rio Principles directly relating to forest management have been mentioned previously. In addition, the Rio Principles dealing with energy and non-renewable resources could have significant implications for wood use and production if applied to the development of 'life cycle assessment' of products. This considers the inputs and outputs of the manufacturing process including energy and waste, and the effect of the disposal of the product on the environment once it has become redundant. Such detailed auditing may provide wood with a greater value (not necessarily monetary) than other materials such as metal and plastic. This may become a very interesting contribution to the arguments that support the expansion of woodland cover in Great Britain.

New planting

In 1994 the command paper 'Our Forests – the Way Ahead' confirmed earlier Government commitments to a continued expansion of the forest area and indicated that grants were targeted to encourage:

- continued new planting of conifers to meet commercial demand for the wood processing industry;
- more planting of broadleaved and mixed woods on suitable sites and the planting of woodlands as an alternative use of agricultural land;
- the extension of semi-natural woodlands and native pinewoods;
- the creation of woodlands close to areas of population with benefits for local communities;
- a general shift 'down the hill' on to land of better quality.

The Rural White Paper (Department of the Environment 1995) stated aspirational woodland expansion targets for England, Scotland and Wales. In England a doubling over the next half century is envisaged. In Scotland a continued expansion of forestry is proposed where the quality of new woodland is as important as the physical expansion of forestry providing environmental benefits as well as increasing timber production in the long-term. For Wales the proposed figure was a 50 per cent increase over the next half century. In England and Wales the expansion targets were linked to changes to the Common Agricultural Policy (CAP) which affects many facets of the rural landscape. A discussion paper was issued by the Forestry Commission and Countryside Commission to develop the debate on the proposals in the White Paper (Forestry Commission and Countryside Commission 1996) and the responses to this were published (Forestry Commission and Countryside Commission 1997).

The proposed expansion is linked to a number of initiatives including the Community Forests and the National Forest in England. Some alarm is raised by archaeologists at the scale of these initiatives but neither will cover the entire area within their boundaries with trees and both envisage long timescales for the planting. This extended timescale may be of assistance in formulating approaches for incorporating long-term archaeological conservation strategies into the forest areas rather than continue the policy of *ad hoc* responses to individual planting proposals which might be quite small in size. The main issue here is not, I hope, an unswerving antagonism on the part of the archaeological community to tree-planting but rather practical concerns about resourcing the work necessary to understand the cultural heritage of large areas within the wider holistic programme. In this way a landscape may be accepted as the 'sum of all its parts' (Fairclough 1995).

The vast majority of new planting takes place with grant aid made available through the Forestry Authority (FA). This is the part of the Forestry Commission responsible for financial incentives, regulation, standards and the promotion of best practice. Grant applications are only approved if proposals satisfy a wide range of environmental and silvicultural standards. These include not damaging sites of archaeological importance. Local authority based archaeologists in England and Scotland and their equivalents in Wales are notified of all applications for new planting. Archaeological sites and areas of importance which can be identified from records or fieldwork are either excluded from the scheme or incorporated into open space within the proposal. Sites within open space present their own management problems but the removal of cropmark sites from arable to allow them to grass over is an enhancement. Subsequent colonisation can be controlled and financial assistance may be available to contribute to any costs involved.

Approaches to archaeological assessment in areas where the record is regarded as inadequate vary across Great Britain: some issues remain to be resolved and not surprisingly involve resources. Generally the arrangements for protecting archaeological sites introduced in 1988 have worked well with many more sites protected from forestry as a land-use change than ever before. Unfortunately the last decade of the twentieth century was not as auspicious for archaeology as other changes such as road building, housing, mineral extraction and agricultural intensification have occurred. There is probably scope for some improvement in the arrangements for safeguarding archaeological sites from new planting. However as we approach a future in the rural landscape where partnerships are going to be of increasing importance, the improvements made since the 1987 conference on 'Our Vanishing Heritage' (Proudfoot 1989) deserve acknowledgement.

The future

Woodland and forest cover in Great Britain today is greater than it has been for many centuries, possibly millennia. It is of varying character, in many locations and is expanding. With the exception of a few, most people have lost connections with the woods in the locality where they live. Raising awareness of woodland history may be a way of restoring those connections and broadening the experience of the spiritual qualities that many people find in woodland. While there is widespread public support for the expansion of woodland, many people are concerned about safety in that environment (Countryside Commission 1995). A great deal of work has been done over recent years in identifying particular qualities in landscape: the Countryside Character Programme and Natural Areas maps are evidence of this (Cooke, this volume). A major challenge for the future will be in agreeing how much new woodland can be accommodated in specific areas.

This may involve increasing public confidence that the many benefits that derive from forests and woodland can be delivered. Some of this confidence should stem from The UK Forestry Accord. This was the result of negotiations between Wildlife and Countryside Link, the Forestry Industry Council of Great Britain and others, and aims to give effect to the Rio Principles and Helsinki Guidelines. Progress towards achieving sustainable forest management will need to be monitored and any necessary changes in policy and practice implemented. As part of this process the UK Forestry Standard has been issued (Forestry Commission 1998) identifying the criteria and indicators to be monitored.

Conclusion

The rural landscape is a changing one and new forests and woodlands are likely to be an increasing element in that change. The last few years have seen much effort going into finding ways in which the needs of the cultural heritage can be incorporated within sustainable forestry. Many existing woods and forests form an important part of the rural heritage and steps are being taken to reinforce that. Hopefully, future generations will realise the benefits of all these efforts because, at the risk of appearing trite, when planting and managing trees and woods, it really is the future that we plan for.

Further reading

Forestry Authority (1994) *Forest Practice Guides 1–8: The Management of Semi-Natural Woodlands*, Edinburgh: Forestry Commission.
Forestry Commission (1990) *Forest Nature Conservation Guidelines*, Edinburgh: Forestry Commission.
—— (1992) *Forest Recreation Guidelines*, Edinburgh: Forestry Commission.
—— (1994) *Forest Landscape Design Guidelines*, Edinburgh: Forestry Commission.

References

Barclay, G.J. (1992) 'Forestry and Archaeology in Scotland', *Scottish Forestry* 46: 27–47.
Berry, A. and Brown, I. (eds) (1995) *Managing Ancient Monuments: An Integrated Approach*, Mold: Clwyd Archaeology Service in association with Association of County Archaeology Officers.
Breeze, D. (1997) 'The Great Myth of Caledon' in Smout, 47–51.
Countryside Commission (1995) *Growing in Confidence: Understanding People's Perceptions of Urban Fringe Woodlands*, Cheltenham: Countryside Commission.
Darvill, T. (1987) *Ancient Monuments in the Countryside*, London: English Heritage.
Department of the Environment (1994) *Sustainable Forestry: the UK Programme*, Cm 2429, London: HMSO.
—— (1995) *Rural England*, London: HMSO.
Fairclough, G. (1995) 'The Sum of all its Parts: an Overview of the Politics of Integrated Management in England' in Berry and Brown, 17–28.
Forestry Commission (1995) *Forests and Archaeology Guidelines*, Edinburgh: Forestry Commission.
—— (1998) *UK Forestry Standard*, Edinburgh: Forestry Commission.
Forestry Commission and Countryside Commission (1996) *Woodland Creation: Needs and Opportunities in the English Countryside: Taking Forward the White Paper on Rural England. A Discussion Paper*, Cheltenham: Countryside Commission.
—— (1997) *Woodland Creation: Needs and Opportunities in the English Countryside. Responses*, Cheltenham: Countryside Commission.
Forestry Industry Committee of Great Britain (1996) *Forestry Industry Yearbook*, London: Forestry Industry Committee of Great Britain.
Harrison, R.P. (1992) *Forests, the Shadow of Civilisation*, London: Chicago University Press.
Lee, G. (1995) 'Forestry Management and Archaeology' in Berry and Brown, 97–104.
Macinnes, L. and Wickham-Jones, C.R. (eds) (1992) *All Natural Things: Archaeology and the Green Debate*, Oxbow Monograph 21, Oxford: Oxbow.
Proudfoot, E.V. (ed.) (1989) *Our Vanishing Heritage: Forestry and Archaeology. Proceedings of a Conference, Inverness, April 1987*, Edinburgh: Council for Scottish Archaeology.
Quarrie, J. (ed.) (1992) *Earth Summit '92: The United Nations Conference on Environment and Development, Rio de Janeiro 1992*, London: The Regency Press.
Rackham, O. (1990) *Trees and Woodland in the British Landscape* (revised edition), London:

Dent.

—— (1994) *The Illustrated History of the Countryside*, London: Weidenfeld and Nicholson.

Scottish Office Environment Department (1994) *Our Forests – the Way Ahead: Enterprise, Environment and Access. Conclusions from the Forestry Review*, Edinburgh: HMSO.

Sharma, S. (1995) *Landscape and Memory*, London: HarperCollins.

Shepherd, I.A.G. (1992) 'The Friendly Forester? Forestry and Archaeology' in Macinnes and Wickham-Jones, 161–8.

Smout, T.C. (ed.) (1997) *Scottish Woodland History*, Edinburgh: Scottish Cultural Press.

Swain, H. (ed.) (1993) *Rescuing the Historic Environment: Archaeology, the Green Movement and Conservation Strategies for the British Landscape*, Hereford: RESCUE.

United Nations Conference on Environment and Development (1993) *Agenda 21: Programme of Action for Sustainable Development, Rio Declaration on Environment and Development, Statement of Forest Principles*, New York: United Nations.

Yarnell, T. (1993) 'Archaeological Conservation in Woods and Forests' in Swain (1993), 29–30.

Chapter 9

SUSTAINABLE LANDSCAPE MANAGEMENT: PEAK PRACTICE AND THEORY

Ken Smith

Introduction

The ten National Parks in England and Wales were created as a result of the National Parks and Access to the Countryside Act 1949 to protect some of the finest countryside in England and Wales in response to the Dower Report (1945) and the Hobhouse Report (1947). The first was the Peak District National Park, which came into being in April 1951. The most recent formal addition to the family of National Parks has been the Broads Authority, a National Park in all but name. As the title of the Act makes clear, the Parks were also intended to provide accessible countryside for those populations who otherwise did not have that facility. Unlike many National Parks elsewhere around the world, those in England and Wales are not wilderness parks, they are living landscapes, where people reside and earn their livings. The Peak District National Park, for example, currently has a population of around 38,000 living within its 550 square miles.

Over the decades, with various social, economic and political changes, the nature and scale of demands on National Parks have changed dramatically. This has been reflected in some of the changes in the powers and responsibilities that the National Park Authorities (NPAs) have gained, the better to enable them to manage their precious landscapes. Following local government reorganisation in the early 1970s, the Authorities gained responsibility for local planning matters. In 1981 NPAs, alone amongst local authorities, were empowered to see, comment upon and, if appropriate, seek amendments to farmers' grant applications to the Ministry of Agriculture, Fisheries and Food, before those applications were submitted. In 1976, in response to the increasing tension between the twin National Park purposes of conservation and recreation, Government advice contained within the Report of the National Parks Policies Review Committee (Circular 4/76 from the Department of the Environment) made clear that where conflict arises conservation should take priority. This advice was reinforced twenty years later in Circular 12/96.

The functions, responsibilities and administration of the National Parks were thoroughly reviewed in the early 1990s (Edwards 1991) and following on from that review Section 61(1) of the Environment Act 1995 brought with it redefined National Park purposes, including for the first time, the explicit mention of cultural heritage. Summarised, the twin objectives are:

(a)   the conservation and enhancement of the natural beauty, wildlife and cultural heritage of National Parks

and

(b)   the promotion of opportunities for the understanding and enjoyment of the special qualities of National Parks.

In pursuit of these purposes, NPAs are required to foster the economic and social well-being of local communities within National Parks, but without incurring significant expenditure in doing so (Section 62[1] Environment Act 1995). For further discussions of the contribution of archaeology to the conservation and enhancement of cultural heritage within the Parks, readers are referred to White (1993) and White and Iles (1991).

After 1974, eight of the ten National Parks were run through committees of County Councils. Only the Lake District and Peak District operated as autonomous Planning Boards. As a result of the 1995 Act, all ten National Parks have been, since 1 April 1997, independent local authorities with sole responsibility for local planning matters, including minerals planning. As can be seen from the revised National Park purposes listed above, they retain their primary responsibilities for the conservation management of National Parks landscapes and for enabling the public to continue to use and enjoy them, whilst needing also to have regard to socio-economic issues when carrying out those purposes.

Pressures

The principal pressures that apply within National Parks can be grouped broadly under three headings: industry, development and recreation. Much of what follows draws on examples from the Peak District and, while there will be differences in degree and emphasis in other National Parks, the broad themes apply generally throughout.

Industry

As noted above, the National Parks are functioning landscapes where people live and earn their keep. The most obvious industry for many is agriculture. It is farming that gives the landscape much of its character and it is daily agricultural management that maintains the familiar and reassuring appearance of the scenery. Manifest evidence of such management, such as enormous lengths of walling in even the remotest fells and moors reminds us that past human activity has influenced the development of what are often considered to be wild and untamed landscapes.

A less extensive but often more emotive industry in National Parks is mineral extraction (see Griffiths, this volume). The very fact that the Parks are almost all in upland areas means that they contain exploitable deposits of hard rock of various types, and so many contain or are fringed by quarries of considerable size. Many quarry developments within National Parks are resisted, often (but not always) successfully, and many applications are only resolved on appeal. The application of the so-called 'Silkin Test', which seeks to discover whether a particular mineral is only available in a National Park, has been a useful tool in the conservation management of Park landscapes. Some National Parks also contain other minerals that companies seek to exploit. These vary in type as well as extraction method and include oil, coal, china clay, fluorspar, calcite and barytes.

Because of their remoteness and the type of landscape they encompass, all National Parks are affected to a greater or lesser extent by the military and the demands that it makes (see Barnes, this volume). These demands vary from Park to Park, but include low-flying zones, gunnery ranges, infantry training areas and the host of installations, buildings and other infrastructure required to support the modern military machine.

In some parts of some National Parks, commercial forestry is a significant industry, whether through a national organisation such as Forest Enterprise or through the estates of major landowners (see Yarnell, this volume). Although not a major employer, because of the nature of the industry, it generates the subsidiary activities of woodland management, felling, hauling and processing timber. The plantations themselves, no matter how well they may be designed, have a major impact on the character of the landscape. The planting, long-term maturation and harvesting of the timber, and the methods used, have a significant impact both on the landscape and its cultural heritage component, and on people's perception of the landscape and the role of forestry within it.

In many ways, National Parks need such industries in order to maintain the land. Without farming, the character of individual National Parks would disappear beneath a tide of scrub. The mineral, forestry and military industries bring investment and income to the areas, maintaining parts of the socio-economic fabric and feeding ultimately into management of elements of other parts of the landscape. This is not meant as an apologia for these industries which, at their worst, can be terribly destructive. Rather it is a realistic attempt to acknowledge the role industry and the NPAs have to play in the conservation management of National Park landscapes and the socio-economic forces that underpin much of that positive management. The skill and the challenge in maintaining National Park landscapes in the face of the many and varied demands for industrial development is not always in winning refusals for such development; it is also in identifying which developments can be accommodated. In this way the character of the landscape is not compromised, and it may still be appreciated by all who wish to view it without undermining the socio-economic foundations of the Park.

Development

It is acknowledged that much of the industry described above constitutes development, but the term is used here to cover such other local planning matters as housing and farm buildings, as well as those land uses which fall outside the remit of the planning system, such as small-scale woodlands.

Some 38,000 people are resident within the Peak District National Park, yet only a small fraction works within the Park. The majority is either retired or works outside the Park, taking advantage simply of an attractive place to live. Market forces being what they are, this leads to higher property prices within the Park than in the areas surrounding it. This has a number of knock-on effects. At one level it means that, given the relatively low level of incomes in industries within the Park, property prices move outside the reach of local families and houses are then purchased by people from outside. This trend often manifests itself in proposals for significant alterations to property, frequently accompanied by attempts to realise an idealised vision of village England which is out of character for the local area and which in reality does not exist anywhere. While the planning process can deal with the wilder flights of fancy, alterations which fall within the definition of permitted development, or which require no planning permission at all, can have a remarkable effect. Replacement windows in uPVC can introduce styles and finishes completely at odds with the local character. The fast-developing 'nostalgia industry' with its 'olde worlde' carriage lamps and other adornments can infuse a street scene with a character that is inappropriate to the area, and can introduce a sameness, a dull and boring similarity, that obscures regional differences between north and south, and east and west. New housing also presents problems. In the Peak District National Park there is a general policy against new housing in the countryside. Development is effectively confined to existing settlements. In this way the open character of the rural landscape is maintained. However, since many of the villages in the Peak District were larger or more densely settled in the medieval period, spaces within them earmarked for development are often locations where structures existed in the past. This means that, under the provisions of PPG16, development must be preceded by archaeological investigation, funded by the developer. Alternatively it may be refused planning permission; in the light of the policy against construction outside villages, this causes inevitable tension.

Small-scale woodland development can have a marked impact on the landscape. Trees are, in the main, a significant element in the character of the landscape, whether through profusion or scarcity. Whilst the desire to plant trees is laudable, if it is done in ignorance of the character of the landscape, the result can be inappropriate. On the White Peak limestone plateau, for example, the walled-up medieval field systems surrounding the long-established villages are characterised by kilometres of walls bounding grassland fields, with trees grouped in twos or threes at corners or individually along field boundaries. Larger stands of trees are entirely at odds with the character of this landscape, and yet are encouraged by grant systems that support only plantations of one hectare or more. While forestry guidelines ensure that recognised archaeological sites are not planted up, recognition of the importance of the landscape character is not yet an accepted criterion. The proliferation of woodland initiatives such as the National Forest, Millennium Woodlands and New Native Woodlands means that the character of significant tracts of countryside, both within and without National Parks, could be significantly altered and not necessarily for the better (see Fairclough and Allen, this volume, for further views on this subject)

Recreation

As noted in the introduction, the encouragement of recreation is a major function of the National Parks. Fifty years ago the main recreational uses in the minds of those drafting the 1949 Act were climbing and, more particularly, walking. Social changes over the last fifty years have increased the leisure time available to many people. Increased mobility, particularly through private car ownership, has made many previously remote areas of countryside accessible. The resulting traffic jams and roadside parking are becoming so serious that several Parks are beginning to consider such radical remedies as the restriction of vehicular access. Many NPAs have already implemented traffic management solutions of various types, whether to manage existing levels of traffic or tempt people away from their cars. These include car park provision with associated works to prevent roadside parking, subsidised bus and train fares, weekend road closures and park and ride schemes. Such measures have met with varying degrees of success, usually with the less controversial being the more successful. The introduction of charges in previously free National Park car parks in the Peak District as a means both of deterring drivers and generating additional income for the management of the landscape within the National Park has met with a response that varies from positive acceptance to vandalising antagonism.

The popularity of a range of countryside recreation pursuits has an increasingly detrimental impact on National Park landscapes. The apparently harmless pursuit of walking results in damage to footpaths as the number of ramblers increases. Improvements in outdoor clothing and footwear mean that people are more inclined to go out in inclement weather, when footpath erosion accelerates. The result is that the start of the Pennine Way in the Peak District has been the subject of a programme of major repairs, resurfacing and re-routeing to stem the erosion of the peat areas which it crosses. Stone flags have been helicoptered in to create causeways across the landscape, reminiscent of those built in the medieval period for packhorses, and for exactly the same reason: to provide a sound surface to use across soft ground, thereby minimising erosion.

A number of NPAs have been able to provide robust walking routes by converting redundant railway lines to such ends. In the Peak District, the closure of the Matlock to Buxton and the Ashbourne to Buxton lines provided an ideal opportunity for such initiatives. These are now heavily used trails with walkers, horse riders and cyclists using them on all days of the year. This initiative has led to the development of cycle-hire outlets, to provide income for the maintenance and repair of trail facilities and infrastructure.

Nevertheless, the recent popularity of mountain bikes and trail bikes brings with it its own problems. While there are claims to the contrary, empirical evidence does suggest that the use of mountain bikes on bridleways results in increased erosion. Their common and illegal use on footpaths creates further erosion and damage as well as posing a danger to walkers. Trail bikes create further damage and pose a noise pollution problem that is impossible to deal with. The increased use of 4x4s has vastly accelerated the damage to soft rural routes, with green lanes becoming quagmires. In these increasingly litigious times, highway authorities are being threatened with prosecution for not maintaining green lanes or Roads Used as Public Paths (RUPPs) when they have been damaged by inappropriate but not illegal use. At the same time, some highway authorities have attempted to limit use of or declassify particular routes, recognising that they were never intended for or subjected to such uses in the past. Such attempts often meet with legal challenges by individuals and organisations that are well-financed, vocal, informed and determined to pursue their right to a particular activity, apparently regardless of the wider impact of that activity. While government advice might be that recreation should take second place to conservation, the reality is that this does not always occur.

Sustainable management: the way forward

Sustainability

The preceding section is neither a comprehensive assessment of the difficulties facing National Parks, nor is it meant to be a list of problems with no solutions in sight. Rather, it indicates the range and type of pressures on the countryside, many of which face areas outside the Parks as well as within them. At the same time, many NPAs are actively engaged in devising and applying a range of conservation prescriptions in attempts to solve existing problems and anticipate those yet to appear. Such strategies fulfil the very nature of the original National Park purposes, as set out in the 1949 Act and reinforced in the 1995 Act, requiring sustainable management.

Sustainability, in its archaeological sense, has been defined by the Council for British Archaeology as 'development which meets the needs of today without compromising the ability of future generations to understand, appreciate and benefit from Britain's historic environment' (Clark 1993, 90). English Heritage has more recently suggested that the central tenet of sustainability is 'that we should achieve necessary growth without disinheriting our grandchildren or mortgaging their future – at its simplest, that the activities necessary to meet our range of needs can be continued indefinitely' (English Heritage 1997, 1). These concepts are already embodied to an extent in a variety of government policies. For example, paragraph 6 of Planning Policy Guidance Note 16 *Planning and Archaeology* (Department of the Environment 1990) states that: 'archaeological remains should be seen as a finite and non-renewable resource, in many cases highly fragile and vulnerable to damage and destruction'. This phrase is now repeated in a variety of ways in strategic plans in local authorities across the country. It is also the basis for such community-based initiatives as Agenda 21.

Sustainability of the historic environment is, in many respects, conservation by another name. But sustainability of the historic landscape demands a wider temporal perspective: it is necessary to understand how the landscape has developed through time in order to be able to take a longer-term view of the implications of our actions. Such a conspectus should certainly be more far-seeing than the five or ten years that most strategic plans allow for, yet it should be possible to incorporate it into those plans.

It also demands a wider spatial perspective: the landscape as a whole needs to be considered, not just the individual sites and monuments within it. Without this broader view the character of the landscape cannot be established and appropriately informed decisions cannot be made as to whether scarce resources should be invested in the sustainable management of one element or another, in one location or another. At the same time, an integrated approach must be taken towards the total environment, which includes the wildlife and the landscape. Note also needs to be taken of the different ways that the landscape and its component parts are perceived, recognised and valued by different people with different sets of values.

These differing values have been expounded by Graham Fairclough (this volume and English Heritage 1997) and include:

- cultural values,
- educational and cultural values,
- economic values,
- resource values,
- recreational values,
- aesthetic values.

In order to accommodate these differing values, greater public involvement will be needed in the decision-making process regarding society's needs and the environment. Such decisions are increasingly based on an assessment of elements as:

- critical assets (to be conserved at all costs),
- constant assets (subject to change while retaining their overall character),
- tradable assets (can be exchanged for other benefits).

Activities will need to be kept at levels that do no permanent damage to the historic environment, while decisions about that environment must be made on the basis of the best possible information.

Landscape characterisation

The starting point for generating any chance of accommodating the range of values that are ascribed to sites, monuments and landscapes, and for assessing the value of the assets that might be identified, is to understand the landscape in which they occur. Any comprehension of the contemporary landscape must embrace an understanding of earlier landscapes, elements of which remain in the present palimpsest.

The Peak District National Park's Archaeology Service recently completed a contract of work for English Heritage, considering the lead mine landscapes of the Peak District for the Monuments Protection Programme (MPP). The work was carried out by Dr John Barnatt, the authority's Senior Survey Archaeologist. This work considered the areas affected by lead mining (i.e. those featuring direct impacts from the industry such as waste heaps and processing areas, and those indirectly affected such as settlements). An analysis was also made of the agricultural landscape, to assess the impact of the industry. This shows that the modern landscape is chiefly enclosed, with relatively small areas of open land. Enclosure has taken place at intervals through time but by 1850 the physical infrastructure of the modern farming landscape was essentially in place. In contrast, in 1650, prior to the enclosure movement, over half the White Peak was unenclosed moorland or open grazing. Heather moorland was common, although areas of grassland must also have existed. It is likely that there would have been few walls, in sharp contrast to the characteristic modern White Peak landscape of limestone walls and grassland, which is essentially only 200 years old. The nature of settlement in the White Peak was also analysed. In 1830 there was an overall pattern of a mixture of nucleated and dispersed settlement, perhaps with an emphasis on dispersed settlement in the western parts of the Peak. But the study showed that prior to about 1750 the situation had been rather different: then a significant area in the south and east of the White Peak comprised nucleated settlement with only a few dispersed farms, while dispersed settlement dominated in the west, north-west and north. Analysis of the distribution of field barns suggests that they cluster in specific areas where people had dual incomes. In some cases these were miner/farmers, deriving an income from both agriculture and the lead-mining industry, while around centres such as Bakewell and Buxton, markets and trading must have played their part in the creation of wealth.

The results of this and subsequent work on landscape characterisation, through an analysis of landscape through time, will enable us to identify:

- regional and local character,
- the relative rarity of cultural landscape types,
- where the best examples can be found.

The purpose of this work is to develop an overall assessment of the archaeological character of the National Park and what makes it special.

A parallel exercise is being undertaken by the Authority's Ecology Service, developing a Biodiversity Action Plan based loosely on English Nature's Natural Areas map (see Cooke, this volume). This will identify the wildlife characteristics of the National Park. Further work will be done on natural landscape characteristics. The purpose of all this work is to feed into an integrated assessment of the character of the National Park, leading to the development of environmental awareness and sustainability policies which will identify those critical, constant and tradable assets mentioned earlier (see Smith [1992] for a discussion of earlier initiatives in integrated management in the Peak District).

Included within this process must be the accommodation of those differing perceptions or values which will have their own impacts upon the definition of crucial, constant and tradable. Thereafter, the methods of disseminating this information need to be developed. This is necessary to ensure that the 38,000 people who live and work within the National Park or its 22 million annual visitors are sufficiently empowered to participate in the many and varied decisions that will be made, each of which will impact upon the character of the overall landscape. Only by enabling people to understand the character of the locality within which they live and work and how it has developed over time, can they be empowered to assess whether their proposed course of action is consistent with that character or not.

Application

It is early days in the development of the processes which will lead ultimately to the objective of empowerment and participation in the sustainable management of the National Park landscapes. However, it is clear that the management tools that are currently available must be reviewed, reassessed and renegotiated in order to carry the sustainability philosophy forward in a practical way into the twenty-first century. In the section on 'Pressures' above, three main elements were identified: industry, development and recreation. In the light of the comments made about characterisation and empowerment, it is instructive to revisit these issues.

Agri-environment support and landscape management policies will need to be reassessed. It can already be recognised that the character of the Peak District landscape was radically different 300 years ago. There remain areas that still retain that character and which are therefore important in cultural heritage terms as well as having a wildlife and landscape significance. Decisions will have to be made about the values that should be placed on them as well as their value as assets – critical/constant/tradable – and therefore how they should be managed. These decisions cannot be made in isolation. They must take into account all the identified character areas within the National Park, in order that a balanced judgement can be made. It is likely that sustainability will require a two-tier approach to landscape characterisation: first at strategic level, giving an overview of the character of the whole Park landscape; and second at a more focused level, possibly parish by parish. Many settlements and many farm holdings respect parish boundaries and it is a land division which reflects the minimum area with which people identify. It is only at this level of assessment that informed day-to-day decisions can be made, for example about which walls to rebuild, which might be left to decay and which might be removed.

By the same token, understanding of the character of the National Park landscape will enable mineral companies to make better-informed decisions regarding their applications, at the very least in assessing what mitigation measures might be required for the successful receipt of their development proposals. It should be possible to make better assessments of proposals for mineral reworking, where evidence for past industrial activity is under threat of destruction. If the proposals are likely to remove important characteristics from an area, then it will be known ahead of the formal application what the likely outcome of that development proposal might be. The decision then lies with the developer whether the proposal even becomes a formal application.

Understanding the character of a settlement and its surroundings, including its origin and development, should make it easier to explain why particular developments within and around that settlement are either appropriate or not. Current National Park policies favour development within existing settlements rather than in open countryside. As noted above, we now know that in the eighteenth century perhaps half the National Park comprised dispersed rather than nucleated settlement. In the light of this landscape characterisation work, the Authority's planning policies for settlement development need to be reviewed. Yet it is not the characterisation alone that influences decisions, but also the contemporary values (cultural, aesthetic, recreational and so on) now placed on the Peak District landscape, as well as the importance (critical, constant, tradable) placed upon it. Thus sustainable management must take into account not only all the aspects of the landscape from its archaeological, ecological and historical significance to the values and perceptions of the community now living within the Park. An understanding of the character of the landscape should enable a more appropriate response to be made to proposals for woodland planning. Of itself, this would require a shift in the policies that underpin the grant system, but such changes could be justified with the greater understanding of landscape that characterisation brings. If the character of the landscape is known and understood, then inappropriate developments become less acceptable in terms of the values attributed and their relative importance.

It is likely that recreation, within its ever-changing fashions, will forever generate conflicts with conservation. However, landscape characterisation should enable earlier assessment of the degree to which a particular form of recreational activity impacts upon an area. This will allow an informed decision to be made as to what mitigation measures need to be taken to minimise or halt that damage, whether the activity must be stopped or can be allowed to continue. Where mitigation measures are identified, whether these be footpath repair or car park provision, landscape characterisation will again be important in identifying the major characteristics of the landscape and will enable values and importance to be attributed. This will then enable the appropriateness of mitigation proposals to be assessed using the same criteria as those for the assessment of the original activities.

■   ■   ■

References

Clark, C. (1993) 'Sustainable Development and the Historic Environment' in H. Swain (ed.) Rescuing the Historic Environment: Archaeology, the Green Movement and Conservation Strategies for the British Landscape, Hereford: RESCUE, 87–90.

Department of the Environment, Transport and the Regions (1990) Planning Policy Guidance Note 16: Archaeology and Planning, London: The Stationery Office.

Dower, J. (1945) National Parks in England and Wales: a Report to the Minister of Town and Country Planning, Cmd 6628, London: HMSO.

Edwards, R. (1991) Fit for the Future: Report of the National Parks Review Panel, Cheltenham: Countryside Commission.

English Heritage (1997) Sustaining the Historic Environment: new perspectives on the future, London: English Heritage.

Hobhouse, A. (1947) Report of the National Parks Committee (England and Wales), Cmd 7121, London: HMSO.

Smith, K. (1992) 'Protected Landscapes: Integrated Approaches to Conservation Management' in L. Macinnes and C. Wickham-Jones (eds) All Natural Things: Archaeology and the Green Debate, Oxbow Monograph 21, Oxford: Oxbow, 127–33.

White, R.F. (1993) 'Natural Beauty: Animal, Vegetable, Mineral . . .?' in H. Swain (ed.) Rescuing the Historic Environment: Archaeology, the Green Movement and Conservation Strategies for the British Landscape, Hereford: RESCUE, 57–63.

White, R.F. and Iles, R. (1991) Archaeology in National Parks, Bainbridge: Yorkshire Dales National Park.

PART FOUR

Integration

Chapter 10

NATURE CONSERVATION: TAKING A WIDER VIEW

Robert J. Cooke

Introduction

Conservation effort in the UK has, for the last fifty years or so, been directed towards the protection of special sites such as legally notified Sites of Special Scientific Interest (SSSIs), National Nature Reserves and Local Nature Reserves, and the reserves of local Wildlife Trusts and national charities such as the Woodland Trust and Royal Society for the Protection of Birds. Through this approach a significant proportion of our rarest habitats and species have been conserved. For example, SSSIs, notified under the *Wildlife and Countryside Act* 1981, cover 951,186 hectares in England, about 6.8 per cent of the country's total area.

Nevertheless, site protection alone is often not sufficient for many species, and the decline of several formerly common farmland birds (for instance the tree sparrow and the skylark) and plants of arable field margins (such as red-tipped cudweed and shepherd's needle) has been well documented (Gibbons, Reid and Chapman 1993; Stewart, Pearman and Preston 1994). Furthermore there has been a continued decline in the quality and quantity of semi-improved habitat throughout England (Spellerberg 1991), through agricultural intensification, development and the effects of fragmentation and isolation. In extreme cases this has resulted in the loss of species from protected sites, for example where the species concerned forages outside the site boundary or where the habitats within the protected site cannot be adequately isolated from the effects of land use outside the reserve, such as lowering water tables (Fojt 1994).

The recognition that wildlife conservation is much more than the protection of the best sites was incorporated within The

Convention on Biological Diversity, signed in Rio de Janeiro in 1992 by 150 countries, including the UK (Quarrie 1992). As part of the UK's commitment to this, the Government produced a biodiversity action plan for the UK (Department of the Environment 1994a; UK Biodiversity Steering Group 1995), which sets targets for wildlife conservation across the whole countryside, not just within the protected sites. This approach is emphasised in PPG9 *Nature Conservation* (Department of the Environment 1994b) which states at paragraph 4 that 'the protection of wildlife is not an objective which applies only to SSSIs; it depends on the wise use and management of the nation's land resources as a whole'.

Natural Areas – the approach of English Nature

Developing an approach to nature conservation which considers not only the need to protect sites but also the relationship between these sites and the environment in which they occur, is at the heart of English Nature's strategy (English Nature 1993). The approach English Nature has taken is to look at the country in terms of Natural Areas. These are defined as 'biogeographic zones which reflect the geological foundation, the natural systems and processes and the wildlife in different parts of England, and provide a framework for setting objectives for nature conservation' (UK Biodiversity Steering Group 1995, 100).

Natural Areas (Figure 10.1) and their boundaries have arisen as a result of much consultation with other interested parties (Cooke 1996; Cooke and Hewston, in press), and also as a result of the development of the Character of England initiative. This chapter describes how English Nature is using Natural Areas as a framework for setting work plan priorities, and also how they may be used by other environmental organisations.

During the last two years English Nature staff, based throughout England in twenty-four offices, have been compiling information on the most important wildlife and natural features of each Natural Area. They have considered what the impacts are on these features and, in consultation with other nature conservation organisations, have outlined what the ideal nature conservation objectives should be for each Natural Area. One of the strengths of this approach is that it is 'bottom up', i.e. the objectives are derived at a local level, informed by national and international targets and then combined to give a national picture. The objectives apply to the entire range of the habitat, geological feature or species concerned within the Natural Area, not just where they occur on nature reserves or protected sites. Boundaries between Natural Areas are not precise; they are transitional zones of varied width. This reflects the fact that change in ecological character is rarely abrupt; changes in soils, vegetation and communities occur across transitions.

The objectives within these Natural Area profiles are unconstrained and visionary; they are not time-limited nor allocated to a particular organisation. They are, however, specific to the Natural Area concerned, and taken together the nature

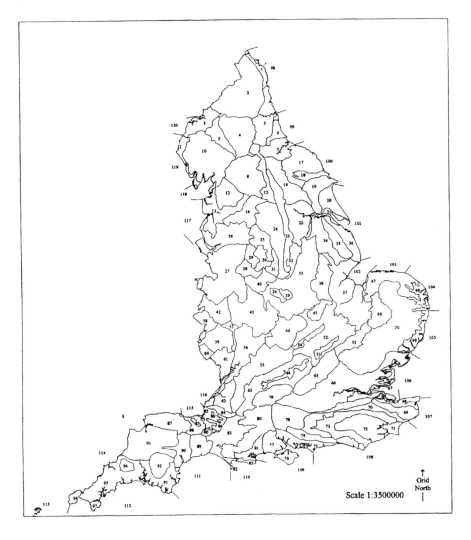

1. North Northumberland and Coastal Plain
2. Border Uplands
3. Solway Basin
4. North Pennines
5. Northumbria Coal Measures
6. Durham Magnesian Limestone Plateau
7. Tees Lowlands
8. Yorkshire Dales
9. Eden Valley
10. Cumbria Fells and Dales
11. West Cumbria Coastal Plain
12. Forest of Bowland
13. Lancashire Plain and Valleys
14. Southern Pennines
15. Pennine Dales Fringe
16. Vale of York and Mowbray
17. North York Moors and Hills
18. Vale of Pickering
19. Yorkshire Wolds
20. Holderness
21. Humber Estuary
22. Humberhead Levels
23. Southern Magnesian Limestone
24. Coal Measures
25. Dark Peak
26. Urban Mersey Basin
27. Mosses and Meres
28. Potteries and Churnet Valley
29. South West Peak
30. White Peak

31. Derbyshire Peak Fringe and Lower Derwent
32. Sherwood
33. Trent Valley and Rises
34. North Lincolnshire Coversands and Clay Vales
35. Lincolnshire Wolds
36. Lincolnshire Coast and Marshes
37. The Fens
38. Lincolnshire and Rutland Limestone
39. Charnwood
40. Needwood and South Derbyshire Claylands
41. Oswestry Uplands
42. Shropshire Hills
43. Midlands Plateau
44. Midland Clay Pastures
45. Rockingham Forest
46. Breckland
47. North Norfolk
48. The Broads
49. Suffolk Coast and Heaths
50. East Anglian Plain
51. East Anglian Chalk
52. West Anglian Plain
53. Bedfordshire Greensand Ridge
54. Yardley-Whittlewood Ridge
55. Cotswolds
56. Severn and Avon Vales
57. Malvern Hills and Teme Valley
58. Clun and North West Herefordshire Hills
59. Central Herefordshire
60. Black Mountains and Golden Valley

61. Dean Plateau and Wye Valley
62. Bristol, Avon Valleys and Ridges
63. Thames and Avon Vales
64. Midvale Ridge
65. Chilterns
66. London Basin
67. Greater Thames Estuary
68. North Kent Plain
69. North Downs
70. Wealden Greensand
71. Romney Marshes
72. High Weald
73. Low Weald and Pevensey
74. South Downs
75. South Coast Plain and Hampshire Lowlands
76. Isle of Wight
77. New Forest
78. Hampshire Downs
79. Berkshire and Marlborough Downs
80. South Wessex Downs
81. Dorset Heaths
82. Isles of Portland and Purbeck
83. Wessex Vales
84. Mendip Hills
85. Somerset Levels and Moors
86. Mid Somerset Hills
87. Exmoor and the Quantocks
88. Vale of Taunton and Quantock Fringes
89. Blackdown
90. Devon Redlands

91. South Devon
92. Dartmoor
93. The Culm
94. Bodmin Moor
95. Cornish Kilns and Granites
96. West Penwith
97. The Lizard
98. Northumberland Coast
99. Tyne to Tees Coast
100. Saltburn to Bridlington
101. Bridlington to Skegness
102. The Wash
103. Old Hunstanton to Sheringham
104. Sheringham to Lowestoft
105. Suffolk Coast
106. North Kent Coast
107. East Kent Coast
108. Folkestone to Selsey Bill
109. Solent and Poole Bay
110. South Dorset Coast
111. Lyme Bay
112. Start Point to Land's End
113. Isles of Scilly
114. Land's End to Minehead
115. Bridgwater Bay
116. Severn Estuary
117. Liverpool Bay
118. Morecambe Bay
119. Cumbrian Coast
120. Solway Firth

Figure 10.1 Natural Areas in England
Source: English Nature

Table 10.1   Examples of Natural Area objectives

South Downs Natural Area
- Restore naturally occurring habitat sequences on downland, from chalk grassland to more neutral or acid grassland.

East Anglian Plain Natural Area
- Buffer important semi-natural habitats from spray drift and localised drainage by surrounding them with non-intensively managed grassland.
- Raise arable wildflower populations, for example by creating a network of whole fields or field margins managed for arable wildflowers, particularly targeting rare and scarce species.
- Create new bat hibernacula from disused twentieth century pill-boxes, using methods that will preserve the pill-boxes as historical monuments.

Border Uplands Natural Area
- Encourage new tree planting and scrub planting in appropriate moorland fringe areas (especially gills) as valuable habitat for birds (especially black grouse) and invertebrates.

---

conservation objectives for all Natural Areas make a compelling vision for nature conservation across England. Examples of objectives are given in Table 10.1. This information forms a nature conservation profile of each area, which as well as describing what is rare and special also describes the character of the area and what makes it distinctive.

In order to ensure that national and international obligations and priorities are also reflected the process has made extensive use of the knowledge of English Nature's specialist support teams, based in Peterborough. Specialists within these teams have reviewed the significance of each Natural Area for the most important habitats and species groups from a national perspective (e.g. Gardiner 1996; Kirby and Reid 1997). This has enabled the identification of habitats, for example, which are present in the Natural Area in nationally or internationally significant proportions. Thus although the objectives are based on local situations and need, they also take account of national priorities.

The objectives for all 120 Natural Areas have been sorted and key-worded using the thirty-seven broad habitat types identified by the UK Biodiversity Steering Group Report (1995), modified to include earth science and species groups. This will facilitate the identification of specific Natural Areas most appropriate for the achievement of individual objectives. Using this information coupled with further dialogue between local staff and national specialists, English Nature can advise on the apportionment of the national target between Natural Areas (UK Local Issues Advisory Group 1997).

The wider environment

Although the main aim of Natural Areas is to provide a strategic basis for nature conservation planning for English Nature the framework will be of potential benefit to other users. Natural Areas are underpinned by a broad base of information, as derived by the process outlined above. Many of the issues identified, such as over-grazing in the uplands of England and under-grazing in the lowlands, will also affect other aspects of the countryside, such as landscape quality and the archaeological resources. For example the destruction of dry stone walls in the uplands is a symptom of agricultural intensification, which itself is a major concern to nature conservationists; and scrub encroachment on prehistoric hill forts on the South Downs is reducing the quality and quantity of unimproved chalk grassland – an internationally important habitat recognised under the European Habitats Directive (European Economic Community 1992).

By using the framework at a range of scales, from the building blocks of the Character Map (see below) to amalgamations of Natural Areas, such as those domi-nated by chalk grassland (Figure 10.2), it is possible to put the framework to a range of uses, allowing an integrated view of the countryside.

Links to other initiatives

The approach of looking at nature conservation priorities using a biogeographic zonation is also being pursued in Scotland, Wales and Northern Ireland by their respective conservation agencies. Scottish Natural Heritage (SNH) are developing 'Heritage Areas' based upon their published biogeographic zones work (SNH 1996), and the Countryside Council for Wales has recently issued a policy document on The Welsh landscape (CCW 1997), which includes reference to the character of the countryside. *The Pan-European Biological and Landscape Diversity Strategy* also endorses the integration of landscape and nature conservation objectives for a given area by promoting the 'integration of biological and landscape diversity consider-ations into social and economic sectors' (Council of Europe 1996, 5).

Natural Areas are based upon the Character Areas of England identified by English Nature and the Countryside Commission (Cooke and Hewston, in press). The iden-tification and description of the Character Areas of England was undertaken jointly by English Nature and the Countryside Commission, with the help of English Heritage to produce the Character Map of England (English Nature and the Countryside Commission 1996). Thus a single map provides a framework in which to view the wildlife and landscape character of the countryside as it is now, taking into account the influences (woodland clearance, drainage, building materials, etc.) upon which this countryside character is based. Character Areas were identified using existing information sources, the knowledge of locally based staff and a TWINSPAN analysis of twelve large data sets including altitude, land capability, settlement patterns, woodland cover, surface geology, visible archaeology and ecological character (Countryside Commission 1996). This analysis resulted in a map with each one-kilometre square attributed to one of thirty-three physiographic landscape types (lowland peatlands, limestone uplands, urban, coastal marshlands,

Figure 10.2 Natural Areas in England occurring on chalk
Source: English Nature/the author

etc.). These various maps and studies maps were then amalgamated into a single draft map which was subject to wide consultation amongst local authorities, wildlife groups and other statutory and non-governmental organisations.

Following this consultation English Nature and the Countryside Commission agreed on 181 Character Areas, including maritime areas around the coast, which share similar ecological and landscape features. Nevertheless in some adjoining Character Areas the wildlife character is very similar and in these cases English Nature, for nature conservation purposes, has treated the Character Areas as building blocks and amalgamated some into Natural Areas. For example, the London Basin Natural Area is made up of five Character Areas: Northern Thames Basin, Inner London, Thames Basin Lowlands, Thames Valley and Thames Basin Heaths. Thus the 181 Character Areas combine into 120 Natural Areas. It should be emphasised that the Natural Areas are combinations of one or more Character Areas, and that they use identical boundaries. It is thus possible to look at the map at two scales – at an integrated landscape, wildlife and natural features scale with 181 (Character) Areas or at a purely wildlife and natural features scale with 120 (Natural) Areas. Short descriptions of each Character Area accompany the map which detail the main features arising from English Nature's Natural Areas programme and the Countryside Commission's Countryside Character project (English Nature and the Countryside Commission 1996). It is an important principle that no parts of England were excluded from this process; wildlife and landscape character exists everywhere, and all parts of the country contribute to the character of the country as a whole.

An example of the potential of Natural Areas: targeting for new woodland planting

In 1995 the UK Government published a White Paper *Rural England* (DoE/MAFF 1995) which stated that it 'would like to see a doubling of woodland in England over the next half century'. In response the Forestry Commission and Countryside Commission (1996) published a discussion paper which looked at some of the issues which would need to be addressed if this target were to be met. English Nature's contribution to this discussion paper included recommendations on which parts of the country have the greatest potential for new woodland, now refined in the light of the launch of the final version of the Character Map of England in December 1996 (English Nature and the Countryside Commission 1996), and the subsequent modification of Natural Area boundaries (Kirby and Reid 1997) (Figure 10.3). The response to this document (Forestry Commission and Countryside Commission 1997) indicated a general preference that woodland expansion is based on Natural Areas or Character Areas, or on more local landscape types.

English Nature is supportive of an increase in the cover of woodland, but does recognise some of the concerns raised by Fairclough in this volume, and also those recorded in the above response (Forestry Commission and Countryside Commission 1997). For example there is a concern that new woodland could be sited on areas of interest, either for nature conservation or archaeology. However, forestry is more heavily regulated than agriculture which has been responsible for considerable damage to sites both of nature conservation and archaeological interest. There are, therefore, opportunities to ensure tree-planting does not cause damage, for example through pre-planting site assessments and the refusal of a grant where damage would be incurred by tree-planting. It should also be noted that tree-planting is often not for a single purpose, be it nature conservation or timber production. Today forestry is a multi-purpose industry, often with considerable recreation benefits (Price 1997). Responses to the Forestry Commission and Countryside Commission's discussion paper (1997) list thirteen benefits associated with new woodlands, with recreation and access, nature conservation and biodiversity and landscape character/local distinctiveness being the most frequently cited.

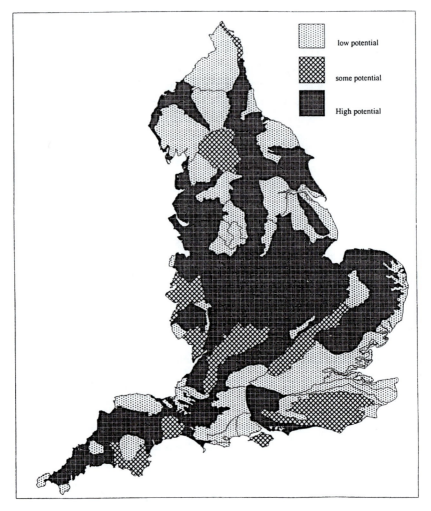

Figure 10.3   Potential for new woodland in different Natural Areas. (Kirby and Reid 1997)

Although in some cases tree-planting may not be well received it is also true that in many cases it is and, furthermore, where the removal of trees is advocated for conservation reasons, for example for the restoration of heathland, it is often the subject of vigorous debate between conservation bodies and local communities. In these cases the woodland which arouses so much concern is not a significant component of a recognised historical or cultural landscape; it is woodland which has developed over the last 60 or so years. Thus the argument that an increase in woodland cover is not desirable because it would not be restoring past landscapes is not one recognised by many local communities. If today we have communities defending 60-year-old conifer plantations on heathland it is likely that the 'new' landscapes of today such as Kielder Forest, Thetford or the new community forests, will be equally cherished by their local communities in years to come. It

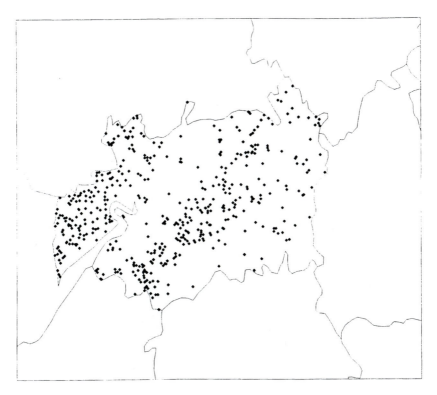

Figure 10.4   The distribution of ancient woodland in Gloucestershire

is thus important that we ensure that tomorrow's woodland is situated in the most appropriate places and is of the most appropriate type to deliver a range of benefits, including nature conservation, timber production, recreation and indeed landscape character.

How far the concept of Natural Areas can help in the process of making decisions about the type of new woodland suitable for a given area must be tempered by the fact that Natural Areas themselves represent relatively uniform tracts of countryside which share similar ecological attributes, both in terms of woodland type (vegetation, management history, etc.) and size distribution. Woodland cover and composition has usually been looked at in terms of counties (e.g. Spencer and Kirby 1992) but this scale does not reflect variation within a county, and may mask similarities between contiguous parts of different counties.

Gloucestershire, for example, is made up largely of three Natural Areas, all of which extend into neighbouring counties; The Cotswolds, The Severn and Avon Vales and the Dean Plateau and Wye Valley Natural Areas. Figure 10. 4 shows the distribution of ancient woodland within Gloucestershire and Figure 10.5 shows the size class distribution of this woodland in Gloucestershire as a whole, in the three Natural Areas within Gloucestershire, and in the entire Natural Areas, including the relevant sections of neighbouring counties.

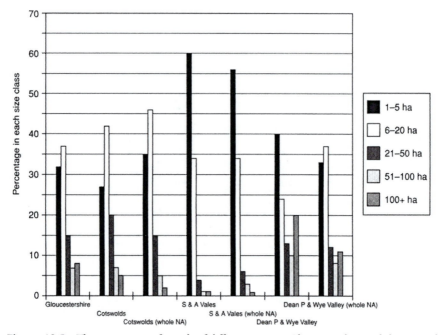

Figure 10.5 The proportion of woods of different sizes in Gloucestershire and the Natural Areas

From these graphs it can be seen that looking at Gloucestershire as a whole gives a generalised picture which obscures variations within the county. These variations are highlighted by the size distribution based on Natural Areas, and if one of the objectives of creating new woodland is to maintain the character of the landscape (itself a Biodiversity Action Plan target and an objective of PPG7), then the detailed objectives for woodland re-creation would vary in each Natural Area. For example we would wish to see small woods planted in the Severn and Avon Vales, and larger woods in the Dean Plateau and Wye Valley.

Conclusion

In 1947 the Wildlife Conservation Special Committee reported to the Government of the day and amongst other recommendations it promoted the description of England in terms of character: 'depending partly on the physical structure of the county, the rocks . . . the sculpturing of hill and valley, . . . the local climate, natural and semi-natural vegetation and partly on the crops that are grown and the agricultural regime' (Command 7122 para 56, 1947).

Fifty years on English Nature may now be some way towards achieving this goal.

■ ■ ■

References

Command 7122 (1947) *Conservation of Nature in England and Wales. Report of the Wildlife Conservation Special Committee*, London: HMSO.

Cooke, R.J. (1996) 'The Natural Areas Approach', *Landscape Archaeology and Ecology* 2: 26–7.

Cooke, R.J. and Hewston, G.D. (1998) 'Natural Areas; a Framework for the Identification and Assessment of Wildlife and Natural Features within Landscapes', in Melvyn Jones and Ian D. Rotherham (eds) *Landscapes – Perception, Recognition and Management: Reconciling the Impossible? Proceedings of a Landscape Conservation Forum Conference*, Sheffield Hallam University, 2–4 April 1996, Sheffield: Wildtrack Publishing, pp. 52–7. *Landscape Archaeology and Ecology*, 3.

Council of Europe (1996) *The Pan-European Biological and Landscape Diversity Strategy*, Strasbourg: Council of Europe.

Countryside Commission (1996) *National Mapping Project. TWINSPAN III Technical Report*, Cheltenham, Countryside Commission.

Countryside Council for Wales (1997) *The Welsh Landscape: a Policy Document*, Bangor: Countryside Council for Wales.

Department of the Environment (1994a) *Biodiversity: the UK Action Plan*, Cm 2428, London: HMSO.

—— (1994b) *Planning Policy Guidance 9: Nature Conservation*, London: HMSO.

—— (1997) *Planning Policy Guidance 7: The Countryside – Environmental Quality and Economic and Social Development*, London: HMSO.

Department of the Environment/Ministry of Agriculture, Fisheries and Food (1995) *Rural England: a Nation Committed to a Living Countryside*, Cm 3016, London: HMSO.

English Nature (1993) *Strategy for the 1990s*, Peterborough: English Nature.

English Nature and the Countryside Commission (1996) *The Character of England: Landscape Wildlife and Natural Features*, Peterborough: English Nature.

European Economic Community (1992) *Directive 92/43/EEC on the Conservation of Natural Habitats and of Wild Fauna and Flora*, Brussels: EEC.

Fojt, W.J. (1994) 'Dehydration and the Threat to East Anglian Fens, England' *Biological Conservation*, 69(2): 163–75.

Forestry Commission and the Countryside Commission (1996) *Woodland Creation: Needs and Opportunities in the English Countryside. Taking Forward the White Paper on Rural England. A Discussion Paper*, Cheltenham: Countryside Commission.

—— (1997) *Woodland Creation: Needs and Opportunities in the English Countryside*, Cheltenham: Countryside Commission.

Gardiner, A.J. (1996) 'Freshwater Wetlands in England, a Natural Areas Approach', *English Nature Research Report* No. 204, Peterborough: English Nature.

Gibbons, D.W., Reid, J.B. and Chapman, R.A. (1993) *The New Atlas of Breeding Birds in Britain and Ireland: 1988–1991*, London: Poyser.

Kirby, K.J. and Reid, C. (1997) 'Preliminary Nature Conservation Objectives for Natural Areas. Woodlands and Forestry', *English Nature Research Report* No. 239, Peterborough: English Nature.

Price, C. (1997) 'Twenty-five Years of Forestry Cost-Benefit Analysis in Britain', *Forestry* 70(3): 171–89.

Quarrie, J. (ed.) (1992) *Earth Summit '92: The United Nations Conference on Environment and Development Rio de Janeiro 1992* London: The Regency Press.

Scottish Natural Heritage (1996) *Biogeographical zonation of Scotland*, Battleby: Scottish Natural Heritage.

Spellerberg, I.F. (1991) 'Biogeographical Basis of Conservation' in I.F. Spellerberg, M.G. Morris and F.B. Goldsmith (eds) *The Scientific Management of Temperate Communities for Conservation*, Oxford: Blackwell.

Spencer, J.W. and Kirby, K.J. (1992) 'An Inventory of Ancient Woodland for England and Wales', *Biological Conservation* 62: 77–93.

Stewart, A., Pearman, D.A. and Preston, C.D. (eds) (1994) *Scarce Plants in Britain*, Peterborough: Joint Nature Conservation Committee.

UK Biodiversity Steering Group (1995) *Biodiversity: The UK Steering Group Report*, London: HMSO.

UK Local Issues Advisory Group (1997) *Evaluating Priorities and Setting Targets for Habitats and Species. Guidance Note 4*, London: Local Government Management Board.

Chapter 11

MONUMENT CONSERVATION IN NORFOLK: THE MONUMENTS MANAGEMENT PROJECT AND OTHER SCHEMES

Helen Paterson and Peter Wade-Martins

Introduction

The advantages, disadvantages and anomalies of a set of policies predicated on support for production rather than conservation measures in agriculture have been considered in a general way elsewhere in this book (see Potter; Dormor; Fairclough). The system has led to the exemption of most agricultural operations from planning constraints and designation of protected areas, but innovative methods of management are being explored. This chapter takes Norfolk, a predominantly agricultural county, and considers some contemporary solutions to the problems of archaeological conservation, and their potential benefits for nature conservation, outside designated areas.

East Anglia is the main cereal producing region of Britain and it is an area where the landscape consequences of farm modernisation have been most apparent. Enclosure, ploughing of commons and heaths, under-draining and marling were all common from the late eighteenth century onwards, but the rate of destruction accelerated significantly under intensive wartime cultivation and the introduction of the diesel tractor in the 1950s. Of the hedgerows in Norfolk in 1945, only 55 per cent survived by 1970. As Potter (this volume) has shown, subsidies from the Ministry of Agriculture and the EEC tended to support production rather than conservation, yet it should be noted that one of the major conservation incentive schemes, Environmentally Sensitive Areas (ESAs) (see McCrone, this volume), was born in Norfolk as a development of the Broads Grazing Marsh Conservation Scheme launched in 1985.

If agriculture has only recently begun to benefit from conservation measures, so too has archaeology. The 1970s saw the rise of field archaeology as an assertive profession, following the formation of RESCUE – the Trust for British Archaeology – in 1971, and whilst this raised national consciousness and undoubtedly led to the retrieval of much information through excavation from sites threatened by development, the backlog of unpublished and inadequately archived excavations has led to a radical rethinking of archaeological policies and procedures. It was in response to threats from development that the County Sites and Monuments Records (SMRs) were created throughout the 1970s and 1980s, formalising the existing records kept in many counties (in Norfolk Rainbird Clarke had begun compiling an index of sites as early as the 1930s). It was in this initiative that the germ of a more conservationist approach lay. Today the county SMRs provide a broad database which may be used by planners and developers to predict the likelihood of important archaeological remains in a given area. This is critically important in a county such as Norfolk, given the low incidence of monuments scheduled under the 1979 Ancient Monuments and Archaeological Areas Act. Notwithstanding the activities of the Monuments Protection Programme, implemented by English Heritage in the late 1980s, Norfolk is a large county and boasts only 337 scheduled sites, out of a total of 32,000 which appear on the SMR. Since coverage by statutory means progresses so slowly, alternative methods of conservation must be sought. The recognition of the archaeological resource as finite and non-renewable and our increased ability to evaluate the archaeological significance of an undug site has resulted in a new policy of conservation rather than excavation. This is reflected in the current Planning Policy Guidance Note 16, *Archaeology and Planning*, yet as Dormor (this volume) notes, since it treats archaeology as a material consideration in a planning process from which agriculture is largely exempt, there remain many entirely legal opportunities for damage to valuable archaeological deposits.

How then might a largely agricultural county such as Norfolk provide for the conservation of its archaeological resource? The Field Archaeology Division of the Norfolk Museums Service is developing five initiatives: an earthwork survey, farm surveys, forest surveys, conservation by acquisition and the Norfolk Monuments Management Project (NMMP). This last, which forms the principal focus of the third section of this chapter, has received the support of English Heritage and is operated through an agency agreement with the Field Archaeology Division and the Norfolk County Council's Department of Planning and Transportation.

The Norfolk solution

1 Earthwork survey

Survey plans at a scale of 1:1000 are being prepared of most of the significant earthwork sites in the county (although for some others, particularly moats, the

Ordnance Survey 1:2500 maps already provide sufficient information). These surveys will record sites of schedulable quality and all others thought to be of local or regional significance. The data is then fed into the SMR. This stock-taking exercise is intended to help the Museums Service and English Heritage to identify areas worthy of conservation, and is backed up by the most comprehensive county aerial photographic library in England, held by the Field Archaeology Division at Gressenhall.

The Earthworks Survey Project was started in May 1994 and 118 areas have been recorded so far. Existing surveys carried out *ad hoc* in previous years bring the total of measured sites to 233. About half the county has been covered and the project should be complete by 1999. It will then be published in the *East Anglian Archaeology* series under the title 'The Earthworks of Norfolk' and will provide a publicly accessible device to monitor monument conservation for many years to come.

2 Farm surveys

The Norfolk Archaeological Unit, which is the contracting wing of the Field Archaeology Division, is soon to launch a scheme whereby it will offer to carry out, under contract, archaeological surveys of estates and farmland for clients at whatever level of detail is required. Most farmers are unaware of sites on their land, since the comprehensive air photographic coverage of the county and the data contained in the SMR remain largely inaccessible to them. The farm surveys will aim to make this information more widely available and to follow up desk-top assessment with site visits and further fieldwork. This will help landowners to understand the heritage assets under their management and encourage their protection. The proposal has the full support of the Country Landowners Association and the National Farmers Union. Time will tell whether estates are willing to pay for such surveys, with or without grants, formerly available from English Heritage but recently suspended.

3 Forest surveys

After discussion with Forest Enterprise, it has been agreed that they will fund a rapid identification survey of the forest areas due for felling and destumping up to the year 2001. This is a significant breakthrough and will allow the systematic survey of parts of the Breckland which were planted between the wars and have not been touched since. It is likely that a range of previously unrecorded monuments will come to light and conservation measures can then be devised to protect them during the felling and replanting process. The archaeological potential of these forests has recently been demonstrated in an English Heritage sponsored report, *The Breckland Archaeological Survey* (Sussams 1996).

4 Conservation by acquisition

Following the example set over many years by the Norfolk Wildlife Trust, the Norfolk Archaeological Trust, again supported by the Norfolk Museums Service, has raised considerable sums to buy sites affected by plough damage, so that they can be put down to grass and opened to the public. Three sites have been acquired so far: the fields around the Roman town of Caistor St Edmund near Norwich (Figures 11.1 and 11.2), a possible hillfort at Tasburgh (Figure 11.3) and a Roman fort and surrounding land at Burgh Castle (Figure 11.4). Wherever possible the land acquired has been extensive enough to protect not only the monument but also its setting. Such buffer zones around monuments are critically important for the protection not only of the landscape character of the monument itself but also of the archaeological remains relevant to the monument that they often contain.

Figure 11.1   Caistor St Edmund. At Caistor, the Norfolk Archaeological Trust has acquired by gift and purchase 48 hectares of the Roman town and surrounding fields since 1983. Although the defended area of the town was under grass, the rest was arable until the Trust put it down to grass under a Countryside Stewardship Scheme in 1992. Annual payments help to cover the difference between arable and low-intensive grass farming, and grants contribute generously to the capital costs of fencing, gates and public access measures. There are self-guided walks, a public car park and a series of interpretation panels. South Norfolk District Council provides a site wardening service. The Trust has won five conservation awards for its conservation and interpretation work at Caistor. Photograph: Cambridge University Committee for Aerial Photography reference no: YI 41

Figure 11.2   Caistor St Edmund. Close up view of the Roman streets and buildings. Photograph: Cambridge University Committee for Aerial Photography reference no: AJI 83

Figure 11.3   Tasburgh. At Tasburgh some of the hillfort earthworks were being severely eroded by ploughing. Since the site was purchased in 1994 it has been grassed over, fenced and opened to the public, with routine site management transferred to the Parish Council. Photograph: Derek A. Edwards at the Norfolk Museums Service, Landscape Archaeology Section. Reference no: TM1996/R/DPN11

Figure 11.4   Burgh Castle. At Burgh Castle 36 hectares of land in and around the Saxon Shore fort was purchased in March 1995. All the land eligible for Countryside Stewardship payments has been grassed over and entered into the scheme. Although the fort walls are in English Heritage guardianship, and have been accessible to the public for many years, there are minimal public facilities and no car park. Public access will soon be improved and a site interpretation scheme is currently being discussed with English Heritage, the Broads Authority and English Nature. Photograph: Derek A. Edwards at the Norfolk Museums Service, Landscape Archaeology Section. Reference no:TG4704/AJB/DQY6

The Norfolk Monuments Management Project

History of the project

The purpose of this major project (referred to hereafter as NMMP) is to ensure that all Norfolk earthworks of national or local significance are recognised, preserved and protected by their owners, whether they are scheduled ancient monuments or not. Grant-aided management agreements were made available to owners and occupiers of ancient monuments under Section 17 of the *Ancient Monuments and Archaeological Areas Act 1979* and the majority of these have been taken up in respect of scheduled monuments, despite the fact that the Act made provision for the implementation of grants to important non-scheduled sites. Until 1990, Section 17 agreements were always initiated directly by English Heritage, but a move from various local authorities to devolve this function was accepted and Norfolk became a pilot scheme, run by the County Council's Department of Planning and Transportation and the Field Archaeology Division of the Museum Service.

Wherever possible, management agreements under Section 17 of the 1979 Act are drawn up between the County Council and owners. Failing that, voluntary management statements are signed by both parties. Section 17 agreements are formal and legally binding: payments for site improvements are made by English Heritage in consultation with the County Council. The management statements, on the other hand, are entirely voluntary and no payments are made; they are intended purely to provide a record of the understandings reached about good site management during the project officer's visit.

The NMMP differs from similar schemes implemented by other authorities in that it is not limited to scheduled monuments. Between August 1990, when the project started, and July 1997 365 sites were visited and of these 307 judged to be significant. The remaining fifty-eight were too fragmentary or had disappeared since they were last recorded. The range of monuments to be covered includes deserted villages, fish ponds, castles, burial mounds, priories, ruined churches and moated sites. It is hoped that the whole county will be covered by the year 2000. Amongst the 307 significant sites, the following statistics show an encouraging response:

23	Section 17 agreements signed
2	Section 17 agreements in preparation
c. 10	entered into Countryside Stewardship or managed under an Environmentally Sensitive Areas scheme
104	management statements signed
50	management statements awaiting signature
c. 40	owners managing site responsibly, but prefer not to sign a statement
6	owners show no interest in discussing management (although one owns a scheduled site)
72	further site visits in hand.

Under Section 17 agreements, the funding of up to 100 per cent of the capital costs of stock fencing, scrub clearance, tree felling and initial rabbit control can be followed by annual payments calculated by the hectare to maintain the benefits of the initial works. Tax-free lump sum payments are made at the commencement of the agreements, which usually last five years. Of the agreements signed to date, four are renewals of existing agreements, previously concluded with English Heritage, and the rest are newly negotiated.

Implementation

Earthwork sites are initially identified using the County SMR in a desk-based exercise. Buried archaeology and standing buildings are included only if closely identified with earthworks. In the pilot area, North West Norfolk, over 200 sites were picked up in this way, of which sixty were Scheduled Ancient Monuments. These are already subject to monitoring by English Heritage through its local Field Monument Warden, so the owners and occupiers were known and appointments to visit could be made. The project is regularly promoted through National Farmers Union (NFU) and Country Landowners Association (CLA) literature and only once has a farmer refused access. In order to avoid confusion for owners, there is close liaison between the NMMP Officer and the Field Monument Warden, and in some cases joint visits are undertaken. These help to clarify for owners the emphasis on management within NMMP as opposed to the statutory inspection visits of the Field Monument Warden. As management considerations begin to take precedence, it is likely that in future years landowners will see more of the NMMP Officer and less of the Field Monument Warden.

For non-scheduled sites, owners and occupiers are rarely known to the County Council and sites may not have been visited for years, if ever. 'Cold calling' is therefore often necessary and owners of unscheduled sites are frequently surprised to find that they have something of historical interest on their land. However, in almost every case, contact has eventually been made and usually great interest engendered. Indeed, goodwill is critical to the success of NMMP. The popularity of voluntary management statements probably reflects an enthusiasm for the reduced paperwork involved as farmers find the weight of EC bureaucracy increasingly burdensome. The willingness of others to manage their monuments responsibly without any kind of documented agreement at all is likely to be an extension of this.

An added bonus in engendering goodwill has been the close link with the County's Earthwork Survey (see p. 138). To the untrained eye, earthworks can be difficult to interpret. After a visit by the NMMP Officer, sites which might benefit from a survey are brought to the attention of the consultant surveyor and, where appropriate, a survey is carried out. The resulting annotated plan, together with old maps, aerial photographs and any other relevant information, is sent in a folder to the owner. This initiative has been extremely well-received and has added greatly to the interest and enthusiasm shown by owners.

Two recent case studies demonstrate the value of the project. In one, a fine set of unscheduled deserted village earthworks was threatened with damage from ploughing. The owner had checked the designation of the earthworks and, finding that they were not scheduled, had assumed that they were unimportant. A chance visit by a member of the Field Archaeology Division staff revealed that hollow ways were being filled preparatory to ploughing. Although the site was outside the area currently being surveyed, it was possible to draw up a Section 17 agreement to safeguard this important site. Ploughing will now take place only on previously ploughed areas and minimal disc cultivation will be undertaken elsewhere whilst the most sensitive areas will remain untouched. Had the NMMP Officer met the landowner prior to the infilling, the importance of the site would have been explained. It was only by chance that a disaster was narrowly averted. In another case, a visit had already taken place, a survey had been carried out and a management statement signed. The owner subsequently wished to carry out desilting of a large pond adjacent to some deserted village earthworks and contacted the NMMP

Officer for advice on the disposal of the silt to avoid damage to the earthworks. In both these cases, it was not only the specific advice of the NMMP Officer that was useful: the raising of awareness of the problems involved in carrying out apparently everyday agricultural operations had been highlighted and the farmers' future attitudes towards their land are likely to have been altered for the better.

Finally, in this section on implementation, it should be noted that the Norfolk project differs from other similar schemes in the establishment at the outset of a management committee, which meets twice yearly. Representatives of the Ministry of Agriculture (including both the Countryside Stewardship Officer for Norfolk and the Farming and Rural Conservation Agency [FRCA] Officer), English Heritage, the Historic Buildings Officer for the county, Farming and Wildlife Advisory Group (FWAG), the National Farmers Union (NFU), and the Country Landowners Association (CLA) sit on this committee. This is a group in which all members have expertise to contribute to the debates which surround some of the more difficult cases. A consequence of this discussion forum has been the interaction between the project and other countryside bodies.

An integrated approach

The integration of archaeological and nature conservation interests, ignored for so long, has been remedied at the highest levels by the 1996 Memorandum of Agreement between English Heritage and English Nature. At county level, cooperation is becoming more common between officers who administer such diverse schemes as Environmentally Sensitive Areas, Sites of Special Scientific Interest, County and National Wildlife Sites, Areas of Outstanding Natural Beauty and the Countryside Stewardship Scheme. The NMMP Officer has established good working relationships with staff from nature conservation bodies and in most cases it has been found that the positive management suggested to preserve archaeological remains is also beneficial to wildlife.

Joint visits by the NMMP Officer and a member of the County Council's Countryside Team have been made to many sites. In one case, a moated mound in an old heathland landscape was suffering from a growth of mature birch and scrub, with a reed-infested and silted moat. Root penetration and the possible effect of windblow were the most obviously damaging aspects of the tree cover, and removal of the mature trees would be beneficial for the well-being of the earthwork. Consideration was given to the effect of the felling on the flora and fauna. As the surrounding land was well wooded, the removal of trees and scrub would not be a major problem for nesting birds, provided the clearance was undertaken before or after the nesting season. The resulting increase in sunlight would encourage the return of relict heathland flora on the mound. The removal of modern silt from the moat, although not a priority archaeologically, would be of great benefit for wildlife, provided that an area of reed was left untouched. The removal of trees was therefore grant-aided with a Section 17 agreement, while money was made available from the County Conservation Section for desilting the moat. The operation was monitored to avoid any damage to possible archaeological deposits. The 'unmasked' profile of the mound and the improvement in the wildlife habitats has enhanced the educational value of the site for school visits and local groups.

It has already been mentioned that standing buildings do not normally fall within the scope of NMMP. However, occasions can arise where agricultural practice may adversely affect fragmentary ruins closely associated with earthworks. Under these circumstances the NMMP Officer will seek advice from the Historic Buildings Section of the County Council, and a joint visit is made with the Historic Buildings Officer. In one case, cattle were damaging upstanding priory remains. A Section 17 agreement was concluded with the landowner to include the erection of a post and rail fence around the ruins to exclude stock.

The Ministry of Agriculture has recently become responsible for managing the Countryside Stewardship Scheme and one of its objectives is to conserve archaeological sites and historic features; this has led to an exciting extension of possibilities for grant aid, normally available only to an individual monument and its immediate setting. Stewardship, on the other hand, may encompass a complete farm landscape and include one or more historic sites. Cooperation between the NMMP Officer and the Stewardship Officer has produced several integrated schemes. For instance, a motte and bailey castle with some upstanding masonry had become covered in scrub, completely masking the earthworks, blotting out light and killing ground covering flora. A Section 17 grant was given to the landowner for the clearance of scrub from the masonry, and the work was then undertaken by English Heritage and the County Historic Buildings Section. Part of the motte and bailey banks were also cleared to reveal the profile of the monument for the first time in 50 years. Meanwhile, grants under the Stewardship Scheme have been made available for further scrub clearance, coppicing, stock-fencing and improved facilities for public access. Furthermore, the opening of a long-distance path has presented the opportunity to create a circular walk. It is hoped that this will link the castle, a moated site and a deserted village, all three sites having a connection with the Cokes, an important Norfolk landowning family stretching back many generations. Liaison with the Footpath Officer has led to joint discussions on the route, car parking, access and interpretation for this interesting walk.

Integration with the farming community has been assisted by the invitation from the Norfolk Farming and Wildlife Advisory Group to the NMMP Officer to join its Council. Farm walks are regularly undertaken throughout the summer months, often attended by over eighty farmers and landowners. These events are attended by the NMMP Officer and provide an unrivalled opportunity to demonstrate the range and complexity of earthworks on many farms, to discuss beneficial management options and to forge links with the farming community. This in turn has led to invitations to the NMMP Officer to speak to local branches of the NFU and Young Farmers Clubs and to articles about the project in the *Eastern Daily Press* and farming journals.

Looking to the future

Two of the largest landowners in Norfolk are the Forestry Commission and the Ministry of Defence. Both these organisations are well aware of their obligations to protect the wildlife habitats and archaeological sites on their land. Joint meetings have led to proposals for a more detailed appraisal of the management requirements of ancient monuments and it is hoped that management specifications will be drawn up for all sites, under the aegis of the NMMP. Follow-up visits will continue to be made to all sites, to monitor progress and offer further advice to landowners when required. Given the requisite finance it is hoped that by the millennium every earthwork in the county will have been visited and management options discussed where appropriate.

The cooperation and advice of colleagues from other agencies concerned with the management of the rural landscape have been a great leap forward in the effort to protect the archaeological monuments in the county. Above all, the interest and enthusiasm of countless farmers and landowners have been an inspiration. The integrated approach is alive and well in Norfolk and long may this continue.

Note

Since this chapter was written the forest rapid identification survey has been completed for all the areas to be destroyed, and the results are impressive. A total of 921 hectares (4 per cent of Forestry Commission land in East Anglia) was surveyed. This produced sixteen previously unrecorded burial mounds, an area of possible Neolithic flint mining and numerous banks and ditches. Several are thought to be of national importance. The forest areas clearly contain many more well preserved monuments yet to be identified.

■   ■   ■

References

Department of the Environment, Transport and the Regions (1990) *Planning Policy Guidance Note 16: Archaeology and Planning*, London: The Stationery Office.

Sussams, K. (1996) *The Breckland Archaeological Survey: a Characterisation of the Archaeological and Historic Landscape of the Breckland Environmentally Sensitive Area*, Bury St Edmunds: Suffolk County Council.

Wade-Martins P. (1996) 'Monument Conservation through Land Purchase', *Conservation Bulletin* 29: 8–11.

Chapter 12

NATURE CONSERVATION AND HISTORIC PROPERTIES: AN INTEGRATED APPROACH

Rachel C. Thomas and David Wells

Introduction

Castles and romantic ruins, located in response to natural defensive or vantage points, have been noted landmarks and beauty spots
for many years. For nineteenth-century natural historians, they
were key places at which to record plants and animals and their
reports frequently comment on the wider geological and archaeological environment (Figure 12.1). Their inclusive approach has
become less popular during the twentieth century but historic sites
have, in recent years, been recognised for their wildlife importance
as Sites of Special Scientific Interest or County Wildlife Sites. We
are reminded of this integrated approach in the acquisition and
restoration, by English Heritage, of Charles Darwin's former
home and garden, Down House, Kent where conservation of the
wildlife interest is combined with interpretation of the life and
scientific achievement of one of the most important nineteenth-
century biologists.

Many early plant records were reported in county floras. Golden
samphire *Inula crithmoides* was first recorded from Hampshire by
John Ray at Hurst Castle in 1670 (Bewis, Bowman and Rose
1996), noted again in Townsend (1904) and is still present today.
Clove pink *Dianthus caryophylus* has been recorded on the walls
of Rochester Castle since the seventeenth century (Hanbury and
Marshall 1899) and special provision is made for the continuing
survival of the species during consolidation and restoration work.

These records are not isolated cases. Historic Properties, the
historic buildings and ancient monuments managed by English
Heritage on behalf of the nation, support several rare or uncommon

Figure 12.1   'The botanists', Joseph Edward Southall. Two lady botanists carry out field survey in Cornwall with St Catherine's Castle, Fowey, part of a County Wildlife Site on the left. Reproduced with permission Hereford City Museum

species of plants and animals and, for some groups, are nationally important. This chapter will describe the approach which the English Heritage Historic Properties department has taken in addressing its nature conservation responsibilities, the significance of the resource in its care and procedures to ensure the continuing survival of important species and habitats through site management. A similar approach is advocated to the managers of other historic buildings and monuments.

Developing an understanding between archaeology and nature conservation

In 1994, the UK Government published its Biodiversity Action Plan (Department of the Environment 1994) which describes how it intends to implement the Biodiversity Convention signed in Rio de Janeiro in 1992 (Quarrie 1992). This Action Plan receives the support of all government departments and therefore, through the Department for Culture, Media and Sport, English Heritage has responsibility for conservation of biodiversity on its own estate.

As English Heritage's main remit relates to the conservation of the historic environment, it could be argued that it should not devote resources to nature conservation. English Heritage takes the view, however, that there is much that can be learnt from the natural world that improves our understanding of the historic environment, whether this is seen in terms of whole landscapes or of individual sites. Sites managed using traditional techniques for nature conservation can contribute to favourable archaeological management and vice versa. There is usually little conflict between the two disciplines. Cooke (this volume) illustrates how a joint approach to the conservation and management of the rural landscape has been achieved at a policy level. Management and interpretation at Grime's Graves, Norfolk and Hurst Castle, Hampshire illustrate how this approach can be adopted at a site level (Figure 12.2). Hurst Castle was built at the end of a shingle spit south-east of the Hampshire coast to defend the entrance to the Solent. The shingle spit has been identified as an important geomorphological site and, together with the saltmarshes, mudflats and other habitats to the north-east, has been noti-fied as an SSSI on account of its geological and biological interest. The land in English Heritage guardianship and the wider landforms at Hurst thus represent a complex of landscape, historic and nature conservation functions integrated in site management. Similarly at Grimes Graves a diverse Breckland flora has

Figure 12.2 Hurst Castle, Hampshire, from the air. Photo shows the location of the Castle at the end of Hurst Spit, built to defend the entrance to the Solent. Hurst Spit is part of a Site of Special Scientific Interest. English Heritage Photo Library/Skyscan

developed in the area of the many Neolithic flint mine shafts. Conservation management takes account of both interests and interpretive material illustrates the
inter-relationship in the past.

English Heritage's approach to nature conservation

This can be divided into five sections: identification of important features, establishing the wildlife significance of the Historic Properties portfolio, promotion of
this interest within English Heritage, incorporation of habitat and species requirements into site management and development and inclusion of ecological information in interpretive material.

Identification of important features

Since 1990, when a full-time ecologist was appointed, English Heritage has taken
a systematic approach to biological survey to establish which sites merit special
attention to conserve important natural features. Winter surveys in south-east and
south-west England identified potentially important sites and were followed by
fuller, botanical surveys of the more interesting sites during the summer months.
Survey of the whole country was largely completed by 1996. Surveys of new properties were commissioned as they were acquired or where significant building or
development works were planned. A programme of specialist, species-based surveys
covering vertebrate, invertebrate and lower plant groups continues on key sites.

In 1995, a parallel programme of data collection from the county Wildlife Trusts
was initiated to identify Historic Properties which were considered, locally, to be
of special ecological merit (County Wildlife Sites) or which held bat roosts. This
was followed up with requests for information from local bat groups and from the
Bat Conservation Trust. Information on the location of Sites of Special Scientific
Interest (SSSIs) and other statutory nature conservation designations had been, and
continues to be, provided by English Nature.

A copy of the biological database *Recorder* was purchased by English Heritage in
1995 to provide a framework to hold the biological records and site designations.
From this it is now possible to make the first systematic evaluation of the nature
conservation significance of the Historic Properties portfolio. Further details on
the extent of ecological survey and the methods adopted is described in Thomas
and Wells (1997).

The wildlife of Historic Properties

Of the 408 Historic Properties, eight are part of sites of international importance
for their wildlife (Special Protection Areas, proposed Special Areas for Conservation
and Ramsar sites), an additional twenty-two are sites of national importance lying

within SSSIs, forty-five have been identified as County Wildlife Sites (CWSs) while eighty-eight support bats, red squirrels, dormice or other species protected under the Wildlife and Countryside Act 1981. Overall over one-third of the Historic Properties support some feature of statutory or local nature conservation significance (Table 12.1). Areas of particular importance include bats and wall plants where the approach which English Heritage takes may be critical to the conservation of these groups in England as a whole.

Table 12.1   Nature conservation interest of Historic Properties at March 1997

Nature conservation designation	International Ramsar, SPA, SAC	National SSSI	Local CWS	Support species included in the Wildlife and Countryside Act 1981	Support 'Red Data' or scarce species only
Number of sites	8	30*	45	88	22

* Includes internationally important sites

The majority of properties are small. They range in size from individual pillars or standing stones, e.g. Eleanor Cross, Geddington, Northamptonshire and Countess Pillar, Brougham, Cumbria, to large landscape parks at Osborne House, Isle of Wight (61 hectares) and Kenwood, Greater London (46 hectares). The majority of sites are less than 3 hectares and only six sites are larger than 30 hectares. In general, the larger properties are usually amongst the most diverse, in biological terms, although the small sites are not without their interest.

Table 12.2 indicates the habitats present on Historic Properties. Ruined walls and inland rock exposures provide the single most abundant habitat on Historic Properties. Historic walls are important for specialised wall plants and animals, supporting similar species to those which colonise inland cliffs and rocks. Two sites support the scarce East Anglian speciality wall bedstraw Galium parisiense while St Augustine's Abbey, Kent and Bolingbroke Castle, Lincolnshire have been notified as County Wildlife Sites on account of their wall flora. At Stonehenge, the megaliths support over ninety species of lichens, including seven scarce species. In addition to their nature conservation value, they create an attractive patina which would be removed if the stones were touched or rubbed too frequently.

Calcareous grassland, one of the most abundant semi-natural vegetation types on Historic Properties (Figure 12.3), dominates the historically important castles and hill forts on the Wessex chalk, the North and South Downs and the limestone of the Midlands and north-east England such as Maiden Castle, Dorset, Dover Castle, Kent and Peveril Castle, Derbyshire all of which are of county importance for their flora. The apparently high proportion of semi-natural neutral grassland is probably an over-estimate as many of these grasslands have been improved for horticulture or amenity (Thomas and Wells 1997).

Elsewhere, there are ancient woods and important treescapes of veteran trees such as at Kenwood in Greater London, where the ancient woodland has been notified as an

Table 12.2   Main habitats on Historic Properties

Habitat	Approximate number of Properties	Proportion (%)
Ruined walls	211	52
Improved, semi-improved and reseeded grassland	197	48
Woodland	54	13
Neutral grassland	52	13
Freshwater	49	12
Scrub and hedges	41	10
Calcareous grassland	39	9
Coastal	38	9
Wet grassland	21	5
Parkland and treescape	22	5
Acid grassland	20	5
Inland rock exposures	10	2
Gardens	9	2
Lowland heathland	9	2
Moorland	4	1
No grounds or no habitat information	74	18

SSSI on account of its structure and dead-wood fauna, and at Osborne, Isle of Wight, where the parkland supports nationally important lichen communities.

Freshwater on Historic Properties occurs in a wide variety of forms: designed lakes, pools and moats, naturally occurring ponds, formal pools in gardens, at riverside properties and in former supply or drainage systems at monastic and Roman sites. All water bodies are used by wildlife to a greater or lesser degree, influenced by the setting and marginal vegetation. Some support important populations of great crested newts *Triturus cristatus* or impressive stands of water lilies as at Witley Court, Worcestershire and Kirby Muxloe, Leicestershire.

Those Historic Properties which occur on the coast support a range of habitats including cliffs, maritime grassland, shingle, saltmarsh and coastal grazing marsh (Figure 12.4). The majority of Historic Properties of nature conservation significance for their geology or landform also occur along the coast. They occur around the entire English coast from Berwick-upon-Tweed, Northumberland in the north-east to Piel Castle, Cumbria in the north-west. Of these geologically significant sites, fourteen lie within larger SSSIs and a further seven are County Wildlife Sites notified for their geology, migrant or breeding birds, or particular vegetation types. On the coast therefore, over half of the Historic Properties are covered by nature conservation designations – a larger proportion than affects inland sites.

Some sites support species which are of particular importance even if the property as a whole does not have semi-natural habitats. A total of 2,700 species of wild plants and animals has been recorded from Historic Properties. Of these, the single most important group is bats. All fifteen species of British bats are specifically

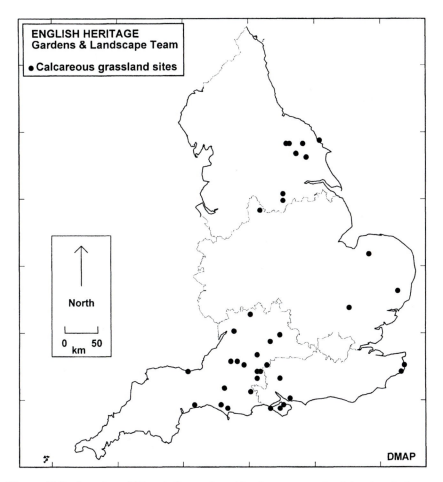

Figure 12.3 Location of Historic Properties with calcareous grassland showing the importance of historic sites on the Wessex chalk and of Midland and north-east limestones. Data from English Heritage biological database using Dmap

protected under the Wildlife and Countryside Act and over seventy summer roosts and winter hibernation sites have been identified on Historic Properties. Some of these are of acknowledged national interest and include sites with five, six or seven different species roosting or hibernating in the property. A number of large breeding roosts have been identified on some sites. Systematic bat recording has only recently begun within Historic Properties and it is likely that there are more, important roosts to be identified.

Other legally protected species on Historic Properties include barn owls, red squirrels, dormice, adders, newts, slow worms, several butterflies, early gentian *Gentianella anglica* and lichens. For all species, the key to their successful conservation lies in ensuring that staff know of their presence, management requirements and location.

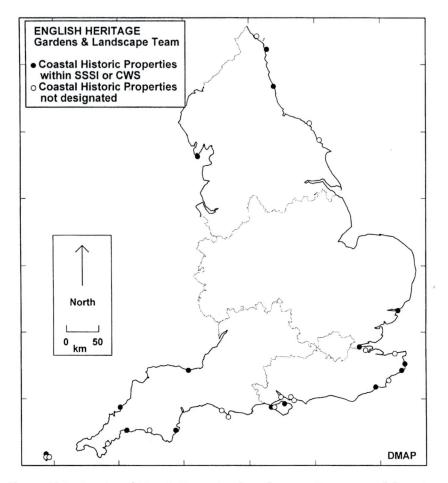

Figure 12.4   Location of Historic Properties along the coast. Twenty-one of these sites have been identified as being of particular wildlife or geological interest. Data from English Heritage biological database using Dmap

Promotion of wildlife interest

The Gardens and Landscape Team, one section of Historic Properties Department, has acted as the focus for all ecological survey and data collection. If the results are to be understood and used throughout the organisation, the information must be made available to all staff involved with site management, few of whom have any ecological knowledge or land management expertise.

English Heritage has adopted two key approaches to this. First, a series of Landscape Advice Notes, which has been circulated widely, providing general advice on nature conservation and land management subjects. These have been written 'in house' and customise generally available guidance to the specific require-ments of Historic Properties. Second, summaries of the key ecological features and designations have been incorporated in short Site Wildlife Statements which can be used by all Historic Properties staff. These Statements describe the biological interest of the site, help officers become familiar with the ecological interest of the sites for which they are responsible, suggest how wildlife management can be incorporated within overall site management and identify opportunities for promotion and development work. The Statements include a map, details of any nature conservation designations which apply, habitats, species and other features of interest, appropriate site management and related issues, the names and addresses of internal and external contact points, the availability of ecological reports and the author and date of the Statement. Further site-specific advice from the Gardens and Landscape Team, or external advisers, is available as necessary, while site meetings, for other purposes, can be used as an opportunity to promote wildlife conservation.

Training courses on bats and the integration of nature conservation into site management, two areas of particular importance, have been run and further subject-specific courses are planned. These provide a forum to raise awareness of ecological issues, for staff to voice their concerns, develop good practice and confirm with external 'tutors' the role of nature conservation within English Heritage.

Incorporation of habitat and species requirements into site management and development

The most important wildlife sites for Historic Properties are those with statutory and non-statutory wildlife designations (i.e. SSSI and CWS), those with statutory species interests (i.e. bat roosts, some butterflies, reptiles and amphibians) and those with other rare and scarce species not formally protected, especially those preferentially distributed on Historic Properties (i.e. wall flora). The approach which English Heritage has taken to four common monument restoration and presentation issues illustrates the integrated approach which has been adopted.

Consolidation and repair of historic stonework

The conservation of wall flora during building work is often quite difficult but at Audley End, Essex, wall bedstraw has been retained on a historic boundary wall during extensive consolidation and repair. Sections of the old wall with bedstraw seed have been incorporated into the new and repaired wall (Figure 12.5). At Wigmore Castle, Herefordshire, a similar, sensitive approach to the conservation of wall flora, especially ferns, is being taken during consolidation work. Species-rich turf from the wall-tops is temporarily removed to allow wall repairs and then replaced in the same wall-top location and orientation. Elsewhere, soft capping ruined walls with turf is providing a satisfactory approach to conserving a short-turf flora and important historic walls.

Figure 12.5. Wall bedstraw *Galium parisiense* at Audley End, Essex. Photograph: David Wells, English Heritage

As a general approach to the conservation of wall flora on historic walls, English Heritage advocate removal and control of deep rooting, woody and persistent problem species like red valerian *Centranthus ruber*, using spot application of chemicals if necessary, but tolerance of many of the small, shallow rooting, wall specialists including wall-rue *Asplenium ruta-muraria*, sea spleenwort *Asplenium marinum*, rue-leaved saxifrage *Saxifraga tridactylites*, wall bedstraw *Galium parisiense* and the stonecrops *Sedum* spp. Lichen encrusted stones, which may be removed to allow repointing, should be replaced in the same location and orientation to ensure that the lichens continue to live in the same regime of light, moisture and exposure. Careful site-specific advice on both the historic and botanical aspects may also be required.

Presentation of the monument for visitors

In the past many monuments which were open to visitors were mown short throughout, regardless of the floristic composition of the sward or the surrounding landscape. In recent years, this has been varied to benefit both wildlife and land-

Figure 12.6 Differential mowing regimes at Kirkham Priory, North Yorkshire. Photograph: Alan Cathersides, English Heritage

scape. Some swards are best conserved by short mowing, but others will gradually become more diverse, or attractive, if permitted to grow long, at least in some years, to allow plants to flower and set seed (Figure 12.6).

Several standard prescriptions have been developed to accommodate the majority of conditions, with careful site-specific prescriptions where the complexity of the site or condition of the sward merits it. Short grass (about 40 mm), cut fourteen to twenty times per year, is used in formal situations surrounding a built monument where the sward is species-poor and growth is vigorous. Medium grass is cut about eight times per year to 50–75 mm. This regime is used on species-poor swards where large areas of grassland or parkland are kept reasonably short for landscape or historic reasons. If such sites are moderately species-rich, the flora might benefit from a taller sward, but in many cases it is able to tolerate these mowing conditions. Fertilisers and herbicides are not generally applied under short or medium regimes except to achieve particular horticultural results in gardens or to encourage fast regeneration where access is especially heavy.

Longer mowing regimes are based on traditional farming practices and used where the flora is particularly interesting or floriferous, or access is low. Long grass is usually restricted to the boundaries of properties, low access areas within more intensely used sites, at the margins of streams and, if acceptable historically, at the margins of standing water bodies. The grass on slopes can be managed as a taller sward to restrict visitors' access and in response to the richer flora which often occurs on such places. The most common treatment is not to cut until early July, then to cut short, removing the cut material after a couple of days and giving a second and sometimes third cut in September and/or October. This mimics the practice of cutting hay and aftermath grazing. Alternatively, the site may be cut in the early spring (March/April) then not cut again until late summer. This is useful where the spring flora is not particularly interesting or has problem species, e.g. Alexanders *Smyrnium olusatrum*, but does have an interesting mid-summer flora. The cut material is again removed when the sward is cut in spring and late-summer.

On sites where the invertebrate, reptile or amphibian interest is particularly important, sections of long grass may be left over winter to provide a winter refuge for these species. This long grass is then cut with other areas the following spring/summer and a different area left the following winter. At Berkhamsted Castle, Hertfordshire, one-third of the vegetation in the moat bottoms is left each winter for this reason. The key to successful implementation of complex mowing regimes to incorporate nature conservation lies in a clear mowing plan which is accurately carried out.

Grazing, for historic, landscape and wildlife reasons, takes place on a number of sites including hillforts such as Old Sarum, Wiltshire, and Maiden Castle, Dorset. At Dover Castle, Kent, grazing is being reintroduced to manage the steep, species-rich, chalk grassland slopes which surround the Castle. This reduces running costs (although the capital costs of fencing have to be found initially), manages problem species and reinstates the traditional management of a floristically important and attractive sward.

Restoration of historic landscapes in parks and gardens

Restoration of historic parks and gardens can, potentially, conflict with nature conservation as many parkland sites have a long-established wildlife interest and, if they have received minimal management in recent decades, secondary habitats with considerable wildlife interest may have developed. The most important instrument to ensure the successful integration of wildlife with the restoration plan is an accurate ecological survey which describes, and adequately evaluates, the local or national ecological significance of the site. This can be used with the historical information to formulate the overall site restoration management plan. Timescale, speed and working methods are critical and an otherwise acceptable end result can be ruined by inappropriate working methods. Instant results are unlikely to be acceptable ecologically.

Sites where nature conservation provision has been satisfactorily included within the management of the historic landscape include Kenwood, London, where the management of SSSI woodland has been enhanced ecologically and historically by the removal of a rhododendron and laurel understorey. At Brodsworth House, South Yorkshire, species-rich limestone grassland flora, of county importance, which formed the formal lawns has been retained by careful management during restoration of the Victorian garden. This vegetation pattern, which had developed as a result of low intensity horticultural management in recent decades and a shallow soil profile, was identified early in the planning process and retained throughout the restoration. It is now managed by careful mowing, keeping some areas short but allowing other areas to grow long during the first part of the summer and cutting in July.

The position is similar at Down House. The lawns support an assemblage of fungi of at least county importance including *Hygrocybe calyptraeformis*, one of the species for which special protection under the UK Biodiversity Action Plan is required. The restoration plan ensured that building access was not permitted across the lawns, that the lawns were temporarily covered with sheeting when work on the house was very dusty and that builders' temporary cabins, which unfortunately had to be located on a small area of the lawn, were raised on legs to allow maximum light, air and moisture underneath to ensure the survival of the turf and its associated fungi. No fertiliser or herbicides is to be used on the lawns and the short mowing regime is to continue.

New development work

The same general principles apply to new projects as apply to routine management. Again the key is a good survey and evaluation combined with careful timing and planning of all work. At Carisbrook Castle, Isle of Wight, major development work to install new catering facilities has been combined with special measures to conserve important bat roosts in the roof of the Castle. The building work was planned in advance with the help of English Nature. Its approval was obtained before the plans were finalised and contractors were carefully supervised to ensure that each stage of the project was delivered to time.

Inclusion of ecological information in interpretive material

Provision of ecological information about a site is generally desirable although there may be occasions where careful wording is required to avoid disclosing the specific locations of species which are sensitive to disturbance. On small sites, or those where the biological interest is very localised, excessive trampling may be a problem. Interpretation helps explain to visitors why management, which may be unusual or different from what they expect, is being carried out. It helps visitors gain more from their visit and improves their understanding of the whole property. At Old Sarum interpretation of the wildlife interest is one feature of guided walks run by the custodians.

Conclusion

The approach taken by English Heritage illustrates one way to integrate nature conservation with the conservation and presentation of Historic Monuments. English Heritage believes that some of these techniques could be adopted more widely. Other chapters in this volume describe approaches which might be adopted at the local or national policy level. A joint approach to conservation is central to achieving sustainability within the rural environment.

This joint approach to the conservation of the natural and built heritage is the principle which underpins the joint English Heritage/English Nature Statement of Intent for the Conservation of the Natural and Archaeological Environment signed in 1992. The annual Action Plan details particular areas of work where English Heritage and English Nature will work more closely. In addition to nature conservation on English Heritage's estate and archaeological conservation on English Nature's estate, it puts particular emphasis on joint policy work in the rural environment including agriculture, transport, coastal conservation and planning. Through this approach the two organisations have published, with the Countryside Commission, guidance on Local Plans and Agenda 21 as one means to take forward joint approaches to sustainability and the conservation of biodiversity.

■   ■   ■

References

Bewis, A., Bowman, P. and Rose, F. (1996) *The Flora of Hampshire*, Colchester: Harley Books.

Department of the Environment (1994) *Biodiversity: The UK Action Plan*, Cm Paper 2428, London: HMSO.

Hanbury, F.J. and Marshall, E.S. (1899) *Flora of Kent*, London: Hanbury.

Quarrie, J. (ed.) (1992) *Earth Summit '92: The United Nations Conference on Environment and Development Rio De Janeiro 1992*, London: The Regency Press.

Thomas, R.C. and Wells, D. (1997) 'Historic Properties – their Wildlife and Importance for Nature Conservation', unpublished report, London: English Heritage.

Townsend, F. (1904) *Flora of Hampshire including the Isle of Wight*, London: Lovell Reeve.

Chapter 13

THE MANAGEMENT OF THE RURAL LANDSCAPE: A SENSE OF PLACE

Tim Allen

Introduction

'Virtually all of Britain has been influenced by human activity' (CBA 1993, 3). Statements such as this proliferate within ecological and archaeological literature, yet it is worth restating that British landscapes have been shaped by the activities of generations of people, mostly for food, fibre and timber production or to provide basic resources such as building materials or water. Landscapes created specifically for aesthetic pleasure may be a particular English contribution to the world of art, but in physical terms they are modest in scale. If conservationists, and society more generally, are increasingly concerned to conserve our landscapes, it is not solely because they provide places to visit, glimpses of the past or a topic for study, it is also because of the characteristics and local variations that help to define our sense of place. The subject matter of this chapter is not therefore solely landscape history and archaeology but is inextricably bound up with them.

Why is sense of place important?

This is a difficult question with no single answer and one which requires the understanding of a little human psychology. However, a good starting point is the idea that sense of place is defined by the specific features that identify the character of a particular area, be it large or small. In helping to define a locality, sense of place emphasises the need to 'belong' which is common to many people and, in doing so, also emphasises a certain individuality –

'I come from here'. It is often a positive influence and, in the context of where we live, helps us to feel comfortable through the familiarity that accompanies it. The sense of pride that often comes with an identification with 'place' is a principal motivation for people to involve themselves in conserving and caring for their local environment.

However, pride can be replaced by alienation where sense of place is associated with deprivation and dereliction. Some inner-city areas and third-world shanty towns on the urban fringe provide graphic illustrations of the way such deprivation can become a downward and destructive spiral, although these areas can also provide some of the most inspiring demonstrations of how pride and community engagement in the local environment can be a force for regeneration.

Rural Britain has recently escaped the extremes of rural poverty and rural depopulation that afflict some parts of the world but the concept of homeland remains powerful, as we see from the annual influx of North Americans and Australians in search of their family roots. Other more recently displaced communities, such as the Kurds and those 'ethnically cleansed' in the former Yugoslavia, may have a more immediate political agenda for their notions of 'home', and their plight demonstrates the fact that the value of sense of place is not exclusively the preserve of the affluent or those with an abundance of leisure time.

Sense of place may also be to used to describe 'somewhere else' or to convey a particular image, for example holiday destinations where our perceptions are aided or moulded by marketing. Here advertisers and marketeers paint particular and often striking images to attract the tourist or simply to associate their latest product with the image. They tend to select particular characteristics and images such as apparently unchanging lifestyles and customs, ancient villages, farmsteads or locals contentedly going about their lives. Such images seldom convey a truthful picture. How many of us can honestly say that in some way we have not succumbed, or wanted to succumb, to these ever more subtle blandishments and sometimes been surprised at the less predictable reality.

This manipulation risks debasing sense of place. It can also generate an adverse reaction, not least where it leads to an Arcadian view of landscape and accompanying constraints on the development of local economies through planning or other controls. Press reports in the summer of 1997 recorded a move by Tuscans to copyright the Tuscan 'image' in advertising in order to restrict its use and references to it to products that originate from Tuscany. Their motivations were partly commercial, in that they wished to prevent a devaluation of the Tuscan 'brand name', but there is an undertow here concerning issues of identity; locals were seemingly tired of car manufacturers (regardless of nationality) using the landscape as a backdrop to convince the buyer that their latest model will lead to a life that compares with that painted by the advert in the Tuscan Hills.

On what scale is sense of place defined?

Nationhood has implications for a sense of place (see Grenville, this volume). Many Scottish or Welsh people (the author states an interest in having Welsh ancestry) have a geographical as well as a collective and cultural sense of what defines being Scottish or Welsh. States are defined by lines on maps. Many of these lines are arguably arbitrary. For example, the Kurdish people clearly feel a sense of nationhood and are associated with a particular area of land, even though that land is divided between modern Turkey, Iraq and Iran. They are often described as a mountain people, a further means by which they are identified with place.

Regional identity also has its place and again is linked to geography even if it is difficult to define. In England this regional sense is less strong than in some parts of Europe but people still speak of coming from East Anglia or the Midlands or the Lake District and this conjures up accompanying images. At sub-regional level distinct identities abound, for example, in the Black Country of the West Midlands or Merseyside. Such local identity and local distinctiveness are growing themes. This is partly about defining individuality but it also suggests a reaction against the growing imposition of uniformity, be it in the clothes we wear, the cars we drive or the way we farm.

What follows concentrates on the regional and particularly the local for it is here that rural landscape management is crucial.

The components that confer a sense of place

Landscape experts (taking their cue from Hoskins 1955) often refer to landscape in terms of a palimpsest – a series of overlays where each successive layer that results from human or natural activity alters (and only occasionally completely obliterates) the visual results of previous activity. The result is an often complex pattern of features based on geology and physiographical features that are altered and overlaid by the results of the activity (Roberts 1996).

In practical terms what are the components of landscape? They can be broadly divided into two elements: fundamental physical factors that are less easily manipulated and factors that are a direct consequence of human activity.

Physical factors

The most basic of these is geology both because of its direct visual impact, for example the karstic scenery of the Yorkshire Dales, and because of its influence on factors such as soils and topography. These in turn impose limitations on primary human activities such as farming and forestry which are driven by topography and soils derived from underlying geology and the impact of the weather. Such influences may be obvious – even today no one is seriously likely to try to grow arable crops on the flat top of Helvellyn in the Lake District, but they are often more subtle and, despite modern land-management techniques, they continue to determine the species of trees planted or farming systems adopted. Historically, these factors have also influenced the design and appearance of buildings because they determined the materials that were available for construction.

By directing or influencing the way in which the land can be exploited, these physical factors still affect the appearance of our countryside, sometimes dramatically but often through their effect on the finer grain of the landscape, for example in determining natural or semi-natural vegetation cover by creating a complicated matrix of conditions each with associated flora and fauna. The plant communities of chalk grassland on the South Downs are very different from those of hay meadows on neutral soils in Worcestershire. More subtly, the calcareous plant communities of the South Downs are distinct from those in calcareous soils on the Yorkshire Wolds even though they have much in common. This last distinction is due to another significant physical factor: climate. In the short term at least, this is not under human control even if the impact of global warming points to serious longer-term change as a consequence of our activity. Climate has a profound influence in dictating the primary human activities that have shaped our landscapes and factors such as the design of buildings.

Human factors

The landscape matrix is made more diverse as a consequence of the interaction between physical factors and human efforts to exploit and even overcome them. The form of this exploitation has changed over time to reflect social and technological change and the impact of occasional phenomena. The outbreak of bubonic plague (The Black Death) in the fourteenth century hastened the already severe decline of rural communities, whose evidence is seen in the many abandoned villages still evident in our countryside. This history of activity led to a constantly changing pattern of land use with each period leaving at least some detectable impression on our present-day countryside.

Agriculture and forestry have been major forces for change. Although being heavily influenced by less changeable factors such as soil and topography, people have increasingly found ways of growing crops and producing timber to satisfy their needs in spite of, rather than because of, such underlying factors. As agriculture, forestry and other forms of rural land management have evolved, they have added to local and regional diversity through their response to variations in local conditions and through established local custom. The result is infinite variation, for example in field patterns, field boundaries and in the finer grain of our landscapes through local customs in designing gates or stiles, or in laying hedges, even if the Midland Bullock style of laying now seems all-pervasive. Form has followed function.

Historically this variation has also been reflected in the built environment. Again this is a mixture of the influence of local conditions, such as topography, climate and available raw material, but also of local custom. One defining feature of the Yorkshire Dales' landscape is the number of stone field barns and many people would identify the characteristic limestone vernacular architecture as a key component of the Cotswolds.

The problem – is there a problem?

If our landscapes are the product of continual change, why are so many people worried about conserving them. Why not continue to allow form to follow function? Does conservation fly in the face of both history and progress, particularly if, as seems likely, pressure for change looks set to intensify rather than diminish?

There are a number of facets to this process of change. First, we have increased power to make dramatic changes in our landscapes over short timescales. The last 40 years of agricultural development has changed the face of the farmed landscape and, looking to the future, projections for new housing indicate that 4.4 million new dwellings will be needed over the next 20 years, largely as a consequence of demographic change. Whilst there is a current debate about precise numbers, there is little doubt that there is a huge demand for further housing.

Second, and allied to this increased power to make change, is the increasing uniformity with which we implement it. As agriculture has become more industrialised, technology has facilitated increasingly standardised solutions to surmount the physical challenges of managing the land. In doing so, this industrialisation has dictated that activity take place on a larger scale so fields have become bigger with the well-documented loss of hedgerows and other features to facilitate the use of modern machinery on an efficient scale (see Westmacott and Worthington 1974, 1984 and 1997).

This uniformity extends to many of the main forces for change in our landscapes. For example economic regeneration increasingly uses nationally, or even internationally, available designs for buildings and housing has tended to adopt standardised 'off the peg' designs with mass-produced materials that are not necessarily sourced from the locality. Recent years have seen improvements here – we now have the cast-iron (or imitation cast iron) heritage bollard and pedestrian sign in our towns and cities. Whilst better than pre-cast concrete or garish plastic, they still seem to conform to a standard design and are the same in Cornwall or Yorkshire.

Underlying this is increased internationalism; the consequence of improved communications and transportation. The result is the creation of world markets for industrial and other products or services. Our market towns now support shop fronts that in some cases would be familiar to people living in America or Australia, even if they are attached to a converted Georgian town house. The question is how far this constitutes a problem. There are undoubted benefits from many of these developments and, in absolute terms, living standards for many in Europe have improved over the last 40 years. Whatever the impact on those caught up in the process, industrial change was inevitable. Economic and social regeneration, for example in areas where primary or extractive industries have ceased, offers many opportunities for environmental improvement as well as posing potential problems if we get the process wrong.

However, there is a growing consensus that we are losing too much that is irreplaceable, that the process of change is not adequately protecting what is left and that we are not putting back good-quality landscapes or new designs where old features are lost. The litany of loss of habitats and historic features in recent years is alarming.

Solutions

While it is easy to become depressed by the catalogue of what we have lost, there are also clear signs of a more vigorous response to what is increasingly judged an unacceptable state of affairs. One of the most significant is the growing emphasis on empowering communities to act themselves, for instance in looking after their own local environment. In Western Europe this is partly, but not entirely, driven by changes in political philosophy in relation to the role of the state and by hard-edged economics. The 1992 Rio Earth Summit (United Nations Conference on Environment and Development, 1993) brought community action into particular focus, expressed in the UK through the concept of *Local Agenda 21* (Local Government Management Board 1993a, 1993b and 1995; Wilkes and Peter 1995). This has at its heart the idea that local people should be able to identify what is important about their environment and then be in a position to do something about it. Its achievements to date are summarised by Morris and Hams (1997).

The health of such community-led initiatives is reflected in a range of environmental activities and projects, for example the British Trust for Conservation Volunteers (BTCV 1987) which exists to promote and facilitate voluntary work on environmental improvement and grant schemes such as Rural Action for the Environment that specifically offers grants to local communities for small environmental projects. Rural Action was set up in 1992 and since then has awarded over £3 million in grants, backed up by specialist advice and training to local communities. The scheme is administered by ACRE (Action with Communities in Rural England), a working partnership of England's Rural Community Councils. The schemes supported are diverse, ranging from 'greening' village halls, to surveying local wildlife, village appraisals, restoring ponds and surveying bats in a disused tunnel (source: Internet site http://www.acreciro.demon.co.uk/raction.htm).

This trend is growing and increasingly National Lottery funds are being deployed to assist. The Countryside Commission has instigated two such projects, the first being its Millennium Greens programme which makes funds available to local communities for the creation of new green spaces close to or within settlements. The Countryside Commission administers the scheme with a grant of £10 million from the Millennium Commission and a further £10 million from other sources.

It aims to provide 250 communities with greens by the year 2000. By October 1997, the Commission had issued 4,289 application forms, of which 409 had been returned completed. 119 communities have been asked to apply for Site Preparation Grants, while forty-one communities have already received their initial grants. The second project instigated by the Countryside Commission is the Local Heritage Initiative. A pilot scheme was launched at the end of 1997 by the Countryside Commission and the Heritage Lottery Fund. If this is successful, a full-scale initiative will be launched in 1999. The £40-million scheme is intended to encourage people to explore and care for the local features that they treasure most. The initiative will help communities across England to identify, record and conserve their most valued local landmarks and traditions. Aspects which are eligible within the scheme include natural heritage, built heritage, archaeology, industrial remains and customs and traditions. The remit is deliberately wide, and the scheme hopes to encourage the conservation of aspects of the countryside that are not necessarily regarded as being of national importance and therefore are not designated under any of the schemes discussed elsewhere in this volume. One interesting development is the possibility of grant aid to customs and traditions – such 'soft' heritage has not attracted grant aid in this country previously.

The Countryside Commission's Community Forests are another example. Noting that in Europe only Ireland has less tree cover than England, the Countryside Commission estimates that 7.5 per cent of the country is wooded, as compared with 20–25 per cent of most of our continental neighbours. The Commission is pressing for a doubling of this cover to 15 per cent by the year 2050 and is developing community forests on the outskirts of twelve major English towns or cities with the purpose of creating attractive landscapes in areas that have suffered from dereliction or major change. These forests will be stocked predominantly with broad-leaved native species such as oak, beech and ash. In 1996/7 approximately 1,500 hectares of new woodland were planted in the twelve Community Forests. These projects are ambitious programmes of environmental improvement that are designed to benefit local communities and involve them in the planning and delivery process.

Building on this community involvement philosophy, the planning system is beginning to recognise that local people ought to have a voice but that this voice should be channelled so that it is constructive and avoids the entrenched 'not in my backyard' approach. One aspect of this process is the Countryside Commission's Village Design and Countryside Design work. In the case of Village Design, the Countryside Commission has developed a package that allows local people to systematically identify what gives their village its particular character in design terms and to convert this into a document that can be adopted as supplementary planning guidance by the Local Planning Authority to help in guiding the nature of development. Although still relatively new, this programme has already proved popular and many villages are either in the process of preparing Village Design Statements or are considering doing so.

A feature of the response to recent change is a general move by conservationists away from looking at special or designated areas and towards taking a more holistic view of the countryside. The Countryside Character exercise, carried out jointly by the Countryside Commission and English Nature, is a particularly important milestone in this respect (see Cooke, this volume). This examined the whole of England and identified and described English landscapes and their wildlife habitats, defining character areas that have sufficient consistency to be identified as discrete units. The purpose is to highlight what is important about each individual character area to inform decisions about future land use or management. These areas are defined by landscape and wildlife considerations rather than any artificial administrative or other factors. They also begin to focus on the fact that the whole countryside is important or potentially important, not least to those who live locally.

There is a growing impetus behind this new approach. The planning system now enshrines through Planning Policy Guidance Notes 1 and 7 the character approach as a basis for ensuring that development respects or enhances the distinctive character of the land and the built environment. In 1997 the Ministry of Agriculture used character areas and descriptions for the first time as a basis for establishing targets for the Countryside Stewardship agri-environment scheme (see Potter and Dormor, this volume).

Given the extent of socio-economic change and of the impact of our activities on our landscapes, government policy seems also to be beginning to move beyond conserving what remains of value towards incorporating more creative approaches. In the last Conservative Government's Rural White Paper, a commitment was made to doubling England's tree and woodland cover (Department of the Environment/ MAFF 1995). Whilst there are sound long-term sustainable development reasons for producing more timber in the UK, there are also many opportunities for combining this with exciting new landscapes, habitats and accompanying environments for people to enjoy informal recreation in a wooded context. Whilst some commentators have reservations about this aspirational target (Fairclough and Smith, this volume) and the current administration is considering forestry policy, evidence of the opportunities that this multi-purpose approach to forestry can offer is demonstrated through the activities of local authorities in former coalfield areas such as Nottinghamshire, the West Midlands conurbation and the ambitious National Forest programme in the Midlands.

A further optimistic sign that Government and society are responding to the need for environmental change, as demanded by the Rio Earth Summit, lies in the extent and detail of the UK Biodiversity Action Plans (UK Biodiversity Steering Group 1995) for key habitats and species. The significance in this context is that the national framework is delivered through locally prepared biodiversity action plans, again reinforcing the importance of local character.

Solutions are beginning to emerge from changes in agricultural support systems (see Potter and Dormor, this volume). From the Countryside Commission's Demonstration Farm project in the 1970s and the Agriculture Act 1986 stemmed the basis for a better integration of environmental goals into farming and farm support policies. The 1992 Common Agricultural Policy 'reform' set a basis for significant growth in UK agri-environment schemes (Winter *et al.* 1998). These schemes offer incentives through time-limited agreements in return for which farmers agree to conserve or improve landscapes, habitats and historical cultural features. Few would argue that these tackle the full range of problems or that they are yet adequately funded but they nevertheless mark a rapid change in policy. Over the next few years expenditure is set to rise to approximately £90 million per annum. Set against an annual cost of the CAP of approximately £3 billion this remains puny but in the context of expenditure on the rural environment this rapid expansion in funding is dramatic. The *Agenda 2000* document launched by the EU in July 1997 (European Union 1997) promises further integration of environmental concerns into agriculture albeit on a progressive rather than dramatic basis in terms of expansion. Behind these European and national developments lie the potential first steps in creating a system for locally establishing priorities for agri-environment expenditure, particularly through Countryside Stewardship, but also through the designation of Environmentally Sensitive Areas where grants are tied to management conditions that reflect the environmental qualities of the area designated.

So where is this pointing? The solutions listed above represent part of a wider picture in which national policy and funding frameworks are set to allow locally responsive delivery in conserving or improving what we value in our landscapes. There is a strong and understandable emphasis on biodiversity in many of these solutions but they are also increasingly reflecting a cultural and historic dimension. However, it is equally true to say that this latter aspect is less well defined and often remains in a secondary role, particularly when moving outside the context of the built environment.

A key to ensuring a proper balance as systems and initiatives develop is improved understanding and information. Archaeologists, historians and others have already done much to aid our understanding of landscape but much more is needed and much needs to be translated into sound practical guidelines for all of those who manage or have a concern for the future of our landscapes. However, environmentalists and others anxious to conserve landscapes must also recognise the dynamic of change. There will be times when proposed change is unacceptable on environmental grounds but many more times when change needs to be directed so that it properly reflects a balance between social, economic and other driving forces and our concern for the environment. The classic example is the Ribble Head Viaduct on the Settle–Carlisle railway. When the Midland Railway Company proposed to forge a new railway line across the Pennines there was huge opposition, particularly to the impact that the viaduct would have on the landscape. A hundred years later the same viaduct was the centre of fierce controversy when the railway line was faced with closure. Conservationists argued that the viaduct was an important feature and that it should be conserved.

■ ■ ■

References

British Trust for Conservation Volunteers (1987) *BTCV in Action!*, Wallingford: BTCV.

Council for British Archaeology (1993) *The Past in Tomorrow's Landscape*, York: Council for British Archaeology.

Department of the Environment/Ministry of Agriculture, Fisheries and Food (1995) *Rural England: a Nation Committed to a Living Countryside*, Cm 3016, London: HMSO.

Department of the Environment, Transport and the Regions (1997a) *Planning Policy Guidance Note 1: General Policy and Principles*, London: The Stationery Office.

—— (1997b) *Planning Policy Guidance Note 7: The Countryside – Environmental Quality and Economic and Social Development*, London: The Stationery Office.

European Union (1997) *Agenda 2000 Volume 1 – For a Stronger and Wider Union, Part 1, Section 3 – The Common Agricultural Policy*, DOC/97/6, Strasbourg: European Union.

Hoskins, W.G. (1955) *The Making of the English Landscape*, London: Hodder and Stoughton.

Local Government Management Board (1993a) *Local Agenda 21 UK: a Framework for Local Sustainability*, Luton: LGMB.

—— (1993b) *Local Agenda 21: Principles and Process: a Step by Step Guide*, Luton: LGMB.

—— (1995) *Local Agenda 21: Roundtable Guidance*, Luton: LGMB.

Morris, J. and Hams T. (1997) *Local Agenda 21 in the UK: the First Five Years: Review*, London: LGMB.

Roberts, B.K. (1996) *Landscapes of Settlement: Prehistory to the Present*, London: Routledge.

United Nations Conference on Environment and Development (1993) *Agenda 21: Programme of Action for Sustainable Development, Rio Declaration on Environment and Development, Statement of Forest Principles*, New York: United Nations.

Westmacott, R. and Worthington T. (1974) *New Agricultural Landscapes. Report of a study undertaken during 1972 on behalf of the Countryside Commission*, Cheltenham: Countryside Commission.

—— (1984) *Agricultural Landscapes: a Second Look. Report of a study undertaken during 1983 on behalf of the Countryside Commission*, Cheltenham: Countryside Commission.

—— (1997) *Agricultural Landscapes: a Third Look. Report of a study undertaken during 1994 on behalf of the Countryside Commission*, Cheltenham: Countryside Commission.

Wilkes, S. and Peter, N. (1995) 'Think globally, act locally: implementing Agenda 21 in Britain', *Policy Studies*, 16: 37–44.

Winter, M. and Gaskell, P. with Gasson, R. and Short, C. (1998) *The Effects of the 1992 Reform of the Common Agricultural Policy on the Countryside of Great Britain*, Cheltenham: Countryside and Community Press with Countryside Commission.

UK Biodiversity Steering Group (1995) *The UK Biodiversity Steering Group Report, Volume 2: Action Plans*, London: HMSO.

INDEX